ISBN 978-1-331-00038-9
PIBN 10131807

Beside the Still Waters

REFLECTIONS ON THE BOOK OF PSALMS

ILLUSTRATED BY

PARALLEL VERSES FROM OTHER PORTIONS

OF THE SCRIPTURES

BY

LADY SIMON

AUTHOR OF 'RECORDS AND REFLECTIONS'

LONDON

GREENBERG & CO., 80 CHANCERY LANE

1899

SIR JOHN SIMON, Serjeant-at-Law, M.P.

Born Dec. 9, 1818.   Died June 24, 1897

TO THE SACRED MEMORY OF HIM,

WHOSE SPIRITUAL NATURE AND WHOSE PERFECT SYMPATHY

HAVE ENCOURAGED THE PUBLICATION OF

THESE REFLECTIONS ON THE BOOK OF PSALMS,

THEY ARE NOW DEDICATED

WITH   IMPERISHABLE   LOVE

BY HIS DEVOTED WIFE

RACHEL   SIMON

March 1899

PREFACE

SOME words of explanation may be expected from me in offering to the public these reflections on the Psalms.

I have often felt that whilst the Psalms are universally known, and form a part of public worship in Church, Chapel, and Synagogue, yet the religious thoughts they embody are not always apprehended. By means of parallel verses, brought together from other portions of the Bible, I have endeavoured to present that harmony of thought and spirit which is exhibited throughout the sacred Scriptures.

Many publications on the Book of Psalms have appeared from time to time from various points of view. Some years ago I met with a copy of Bishop Horne's 'Commentary on the Psalms.' It was published in one large volume in the year 1746. The object of that 'Commentary' was (to use his own words) 'to illustrate their application to the Messiah, the Church, and to individuals as members of the Church, and to render the use of the Psalms pleasing to all orders and degrees of Christians.'

That has appeared to me a limited application. The Psalms are capable of appealing in the widest sense to every type of individual character.

I trust that the use of this volume may help to illustrate the true spirit of religion, and of that perfect faith in God which is the greatest need of men and women throughout their earthly pilgrimage.

RACHEL SIMON.

CONTENTS

Beside the Still Waters

Psalm I

(Six Verses)

This short Psalm gives expression to the contrast between the ' godly '
and the 'ungodly' man.   The godly man makes the law of God his
delight ;   he is compared to the 'tree' that is planted by the 'rivers
of water,' whose leaf shall not wither, for the Lord knoweth the   3
righteous.   He is not found in the 'assembly of the scornful ! '   How   6
great the contrast with the ungodly man, who stands outside the ' congregation of the righteous ! '   Such a life is worth no more than the   5
' chaff, which the wind driveth away.'

PARALLEL VERSES

' For I know him, that he will command his children and his house-   Gen. xviii. 20.
hold after him, and they shall keep the way of the Lord, to do justice
and judgment.'

'That thou mayest love the Lord thy God, and that thou mayest   Deut. xx.\ 30.
obey His voice, and that thou mayest cleave unto Him : for He is thy
life and the length of thy days.'

'An ungodly man diggeth up evil ; and in his lips is a burning   Prov. xvi. 27.
fire.'

'An ungodly witness scorneth judgment.'   Prov. xix. 28.

Isa. xxviii. 14.

'Wherefore, hear the word of the Lord, ye scornful men, that rule the people'; then follows a severe reproof to those who 'sit in the seat of the scornful.'

Malachi ii. 15, 16.

Malachi severely rebukes the ungodly man. In this chapter he refers to a 'godly seed,' adding these words : 'Take heed to your spirit, that ye deal not treacherously.'

Psalm II

Verses

(*Twelve Verses*)

The Psalmist expresses an indignant protest against the heathen kings who are at enmity with him, the 'anointed' of the Lord. He declares the 'decree' concerning Israel, whom he designates as the son

10

of God ; his throne is upon the 'holy hill of Zion.' He appeals to other

11

kings, and to the judges of the earth to be 'wise' and 'instructed,' to

12

serve the Lord, and to make peace with him, for his inheritance is from

8

God, for God says : 'I shall give thee the heathen for thine inheritance, and the uttermost parts of the earth for thy possession.'

PARALLEL VERSES

Exodus iv. 22, 23.

'Israel is my son, even my first-born, and I say unto thee, Let my son go, that he may serve me.'

1 Sam. ii. 10.

'The adversaries of the Lord shall be broken to pieces, out of heaven shall He thunder upon them ; the Lord shall judge the ends of the earth ; and He shall give strength unto His king, and exalt the horn of His "anointed."'

1 Sam. xvi. 12 13.

The event of the anointing of David is told in the first book of Samuel. The words, 'kiss the son,' express a condition of peace with Israel.

Hosea xi. 1.

'When Israel was a child then I loved him, and called my son out of Egypt.'

Psalm III

Verses

(*Eight Verses*)

The Psalmist contemplates with calm dignity the 'ten thousands of people' who have risen up against him, many of whom think that there

2

is 'no help for him in God.' He is surrounded by his enemies,

Verses

but he is absolutely fearless ; he says : 'I will not be afraid of ten   6
thousand of people.' He knows that God is his 'shield,' his 'glory,'
and his sustaining power ; he lifts up his voice in prayer, and sleeps in   3
peace of mind : 'I laid me down and slept, I awaked ; for the Lord   4
sustained me.' He exclaims : 'Salvation belongeth unto the Lord ;   5
thy blessing is upon thy people.'   8

PARALLEL VERSES

'   The word of the Lord came unto Abram in a vision, saying, Gen. xv. 1.
'Fear not, Abram ; I am thy shield, and thy exceeding great reward.'

'The Eternal God is thy refuge, and underneath are the everlasting Deut. xxxiii.
arms.   Happy art thou, O Israel ; . . . . the shield of thy help.'   27, 29.

'Behold, God is my salvation, I will trust and not be afraid ; for Isaiah xii. 2.
the Lord Jehovah is my strength and my song.'

'Truly, in the Lord our God is the salvation of Israel.'   Jer. iii, 23.

Psalm IV
(*Eight Verses*)

Verses

The Psalmist expatiates on the importance of reflection in seasons
of adversity ; he knows that it is in God only that peace and comfort
are possible.

When through distress of mind the night's sleep is disturbed, he   4
says : 'Commune with your own heart upon your bed.'

There are many who ask the question, 'Who will show us any   6
good ?' The answer is at hand : that by the 'light of God's countenance' we experience more 'gladness of heart' than in times of material   7
prosperity ; such as when our 'corn and our wine increase.' With   8
these reflections the Psalmist says : 'I will both lay me down in peace
and sleep ; for Thou only makest me to dwell in safety.'

PARALLEL VERSES

'When a man's ways please the Lord, he maketh even his enemies Prov. xvi. 7.
to be at peace with him.'

'The spirit of man is the candle of the Lord, searching all the Prov. xx. 27.
inward parts.'

D 2

Eccles. vii.   'In the day of prosperity be joyful, but in the day of adversity consider.   '

Haggai i. 5.   '   Thus saith the Lord of hosts ; consider your ways.'

Sam. iii. 40.   '   Let us search and try our ways, and turn again to the Lord.

Psalm V
(*Twelve Verses*)

Verses

1   This is a morning prayer and meditation.   'My voice shalt Thou hear in the morning, O Lord ; in the morning will I direct my prayer

8   unto Thee, and will look up.'   The Psalmist prays for guidance, and

11   that his path may be made clear before him ; he prays also that every

12   one may rejoice who trusts in God ; because God will 'bless the righteous,' and will 'compass him as with a shield.'

Parallel Verses

Job xxxviii. 7.   'When the morning stars sang together, all the sons of God shouted for joy.'

Eccles. xi. 6.   'In the morning sow thy seed.'

Isa. xxxiii. 2.   'O Lord, be gracious unto us, we have waited for Thee ; be Thou their arm every morning, our salvation also in the time of trouble.'

Hosea vi. 3.   'Then shall we know if we follow on to know the Lord ; His going forth is prepared as the morning.'

Zeph. iii. 5.   'The just Lord is in the midst thereof ; He will not do iniquity ; every morning doth He bring His judgment to light, He faileth not ; but the unjust knoweth no shame.'

Note.—Throughout the Scriptures the morning has always been the season for joyous hope.   'Weeping may endure for a night, but joy cometh in the morning' (Ps. xxx. 5).

Psalm VI
(*Ten Verses*)

Verses

2   The Psalmist prays to God for mercy, because of his personal

3   sufferings, both of body and soul.   His soul is 'sore vexed,' and he

6   prays for its deliverance ; he is 'weary' with groaning all the night

7   through ; his couch is watered by his tears, so great is his grief.   His

8   faith revives, for 'the Lord hath heard the voice of my weeping ; He

9   hath heard my supplication ; the Lord will receive my prayer.'

He indignantly reproves all the workers of iniquity; such are his enemies.

PARALLEL VERSES

'Evil men understand not judgment, but they that seek the Lord understand all things.' Job xxviii. 5.

'There is no darkness nor shadow of death, where the workers of iniquity may hide themselves.' Job xxxiv. 22.

'The Lord will not cast off for ever. . . . Though He cause grief, yet will He have compassion according to the multitude of His mercies.' Lamen. of Jer. iii. 31, 32.

'O Lord, Thou hast pleaded the causes of my soul; Thou hast redeemed my life. O Lord, Thou hast seen my wrong; judge Thou my cause.' Lamen. of Jer. iii. 58, 59.

Psalm VII

(*Seventeen Verses*)

Verses

The Psalmist submits himself absolutely to the judgment and justice of God. 'If I have done this, if there be iniquity in my hands,' then will he submit to his punishment at the hands of the enemy. He prays for God's judgment, 'according to my righteousness, and according to my integrity that is in me.'

3

5, 6

8

He declares that he has returned good for evil.

He prays that the wickedness of the wicked may come to an end; and that the just may be established: for 'the righteous God trieth the hearts and the reins'; therefore his 'defence is of God,' which saveth the upright in heart. 'God judgeth the righteous,' and is 'angry with the wicked' every day; his 'mischief will return upon his own head.' In conclusion, he says: 'I will praise the Lord according to His righteousness, and will sing praise to the name of the Lord Most High.'

10

11

16

17

The study of this Psalm is very important, because much of the sufferings of life arises from the false judgments of our fellow-men; but there is a judgment for each one of us, beyond the reach of human sight, seen only through the light of God's countenance, penetrating our inner life, so that those who trust in God will not be crushed in spirit, but will rise to the knowledge of God, and will 'rest in the Lord.'

PARALLEL VERSES

Prov. i.
In the opening chapter of the book of Proverbs are these words ·
'The proverbs of Solomon, the son of David, king of Israel, ... to receive the instruction of wisdom, justice, and judgment and equity.

Prov. xxi. 15.
'It is joy to the just to do judgment.'

Prov. xxxi. 9.
'Evil men understand not judgment.'

Prov. xxviii. 5.
'Judge righteously.'

Lev. xix. 35.
'Ye shall do no unrighteousness in judgment.'

Deut. xvi. 18-20.
' . . . . That which is altogether just shalt thou follow.'

2 Chron. xix. 6.
Jehoshaphat said to the judges: 'Take heed what ye do; for ye judge not for man, but for the Lord, who is with you in judgment.'

2 Sam. xxiii. 1-3.
The last words that King David spoke were these : . . . . 'He that ruleth over men must be just, ruling in the fear of God.'

Isa. lvi. 1.
'Thus saith the Lord, Keep ye judgment and do justice.'

Micah vi. 8.
'. . . . Do justly, love mercy, and walk humbly with thy God.'

Zech. vii. 9, 10.
'Thus speaketh the Lord of hosts, saying, Execute true judgment, and shew mercy and compassions, every man to his brother, ... and let none of you imagine evil against your brother in your heart.'

NOTE.—These few parallel verses will suffice to show that when the spirit of the Bible is more universally studied, then may we hope for 'peace on earth' and 'good will' among men.

Psalm VIII

Verses
(Nine Verses)

This Psalm describes the glory of God in His works, and in His love to man, whom He has exalted. 'For Thou hast made him a little lower than the angels, and hast crowned him with glory and honour.' All creation is under God's dominion, yet, when the Psalmist contemplates the firmament, the moon, and the stars, which He has ordained, the writer exclaims : 'What is man, and the son of man, that Thou visitest him ?' 'O Lord our Lord, how excellent is Thy name in all the earth !'

5

6

3

4

PARALLEL VERSES

1 Kings viii. 23.
'There is no God like Thee in heaven above or on earth beneath.'

1 Kings viii. 27.
'But will God indeed dwell on the earth ? behold, the heaven and heaven of heavens cannot contain Thee.'

' . . . . That all the people of the earth may know that the Lord is God, and that there is none else.' 1 Kings viii. 60.

' Is not God in the height of heaven ? and behold the height of the stars, how high they are ! ' Job xxii. 12.

'Sing unto the Lord ; for He hath done excellent things : this is known in all the earth.' Isa. xii. 5.

'Let them give glory unto the Lord, and declare His praise in the islands.' Isaiah xlii. 12.

'. . For I am God, and not man ; the Holy One in the midst of thee.' Hosea xi. 9.

' He is not a man, as I am, that I should answer Him.' Job ix. 32.

Psalm IX

(*Twenty Verses*) Verses

This is a joyous hymn of praise. It would seem to have been written to celebrate some great national victory, rather than upon an occasion personal to the Psalmist, who says : 'I will praise Thee, O Lord, with my whole heart ; I will shew forth all Thy marvellous works ; I will be glad and rejoice in Thee ; I will sing praise to Thy name, O Thou Most High.' 1

'Thou hast maintained my right and my cause.'

The Psalmist believes that God will judge the world in righteousness, and minister judgment in uprightness. 8

'He will also be a refuge for the oppressed, a refuge in times of trouble.' 9

' And they that know Thy name will put their trust in Thee : for Thou, Lord, hast not forsaken them that seek Thee.　　He forgetteth not the cry of the humble.' 10

'The needy shall not always be forgotten : the expectation of the poor shall not perish for ever.' 18

'Arise, O Lord ; let not man prevail ; . .　　that the nations may *know themselves* to be *but men*.' 19

PARALLEL VERSES

' The Eternal God is my refuge.' Deut. xxxiii. 27.

Let men say among the nations, The Lord reigneth ' 1 Chron. xvi. 31.

Prov. xxiii. 18. 'Thine expectation shall not be cut off.'

2 Sam. xxii. 33. 'God is my strength and power.'

1 Chron. xvi. 11. 'Seek the Lord and His strength, seek His face continually.'

Neh. viii. 10. 'The joy of the Lord is your strength.'

Isa. xii. 2. 'The Lord Jehovah is my strength and my song.'

Isa. xxv. 4. 'Thou hast been a strength to the poor, a strength to the needy in his distress, a refuge from the storm.'

Jer. xvi. 19. 'O Lord, my strength and my fortress, and my refuge in the day of affliction.'

Prov. xviii. 10. 'The name of the Lord is a strong tower ; the righteous runneth into it, and is safe.'

Psalm X

(*Eighteen Verses*)

Verses

The Psalmist utters a denunciation against the pride of the wicked

2   man.   He attributes the miseries of life, oppression and persecution, to

3   which the helpless are subject, to the godless among men.

6   'He (the wicked man) hath said in his heart : I shall not be moved ; for I shall never be in adversity.'

'His mouth is full of cursing, and deceit, and fraud : under his tongue is mischief and vanity '; he is against the innocent and the poor.   Like a

8   lion in his den he waits secretly to catch the poor in his net ; he believes that God will never see it, nor require it of him.   The Psalmist exclaims :

12   'Arise, O Lord ; O God, lift up Thine hand ; forget not the humble.'

14   'Thou hast seen it. . . . The poor committeth himself unto Thee ; Thou art the helper of the fatherless.'

18   'To judge the fatherless and the oppressed, that the man of the earth may no more oppress.'

PARALLEL VERSES

Exod. xxii. 22. 'Ye shall not afflict any widow or fatherless child.'

Exod. xxii. 23. 'If thou afflict them in any wise, and they cry at all unto Me, I will surely hear their cry.'

Deut. x. 18. God 'doth execute the judgment of the fatherless and widow, and loveth the stranger.'

'God is mighty and despiseth not any.' He 'giveth right to the Job xxxvi. 5, 6
poor.'

God ' will establish the border of the widow.' Prov. xv. 25.

Isaiah, severely reproving the wickedness of princes, says : 'They Isaiah i. 23.
judge not the fatherless, neither doth the cause of the widow come
unto them.'

'What mean ye, ... that ye grind the faces of the poor ? saith the Isa. iii. 15.
Lord God of hosts.'

' Thou hast been a strength to the poor, a strength to the needy in Isa. xxv. 4.
his distress, a refuge from the storm, a shadow from the heat.'

' Leave thy fatherless children, I will preserve them alive ; and let Jer. xlix. 11.
thy widows trust in Me.'

'In Thee the fatherless findeth mercy.' Hosea xiv. 3.

Malachi (the last of the prophets), who lived about 397 years before the
Christian era, says : 'I will come near to you to judgment, ... against Malachi iii. 5.
false swearers, and against those that oppress the hireling in his wages,
the widow, and the fatherless, and that turn aside the stranger *from his
right*, and fear not Me, saith the Lord of hosts.'

' For I am the Lord, I change not, therefore ye sons of Jacob are Malachi iii. 6.
not consumed.'

Psalm XI

(*Seven Verses*)

The Psalmist is resolved to trust in God, even under the most
trying conditions, because he believes that whilst God's ' throne is in
heaven,' yet His eyes are continually upon the 'children of men.'
Not only does He witness their actions, but He sees the secret motive
of every action. The best people are often more tried than others, but
the 'righteous Lord loveth righteousness.' The Divine purpose is,
therefore, one of discipline ; this theory is in harmony with the teach-
ings of Moses and all the prophets.

PARALLEL VERSES

' And He humbled thee and suffered thee to hunger, . . that He Deut viii. 3
might make thee know that man doth not live by bread only, but by
every word that proceedeth out of the mouth of the Lord doth man
live.'

2 Chron. xvi. 9.   'The eyes of the Lord run to and fro throughout the whole earth, to shew Himself strong in behalf of them whose heart is perfect towards Him.'

Job vi. 17.   'Happy is the man whom God correcteth ; therefore despise not thou the chastening of the Almighty.'

Job xxiii. 10.   'When He hath tried me, I shall come forth as gold.'

Prov. iii. 2, 12.   'My son, despise not the chastening of the Lord; neither be weary of His correction ; for whom the Lord loveth, He correcteth ; even as a father, the son in whom he delighteth.'

NOTE.—Illustrations of this Psalm are too numerous for entry here.

Psalm XII

Verses   (*Eight Verses*)

The Psalmist is saddened because of the unfaithfulness of his friends, and the vanity and shallowness of human life generally. When men fail to recognise a Power higher than their own, they become arrogant ; they imagine that because their 'lips' are their own, they

4   may say what they please, and exclaim, 'Who is lord over us?' The natural result of this condition is that we find some of the 'vilest men are exalted,' but the 'sighs' of the 'needy' and 'oppressed' are heard.

6   The 'words of the Lord are pure words.'

PARALLEL VERSES

Exodus ii. 23.   The children of Israel sighed by reason of the bondage, and they cried, and their cry came up 'unto God by reason of the bondage.'

Isa. xxv. 4.   'Thou hast been a strength to the poor, and strength to the needy in his distress, a refuge from the storm, a shadow from the heat, when the blast of the terrible ones is as a storm against the wall.'

Isa. xxx. 18.   'The Lord is a God of judgment: blessed are all they that wait for Him.'

Psalm XIII

(*Six Verses*)

Through protracted sorrow the Psalmist becomes disheartened, but he soon recovers his hope when he calls to mind his faith in God

Thus he exclaims, 'My heart shall rejoice in Thy salvation.' This was the faith of his 'fathers.'

PARALLEL VERSES

'And Moses said unto the people, Fear ye not; stand still and see   Exodus xiv. 13. the salvation of the Lord.'

'Sing unto the Lord, all the earth; shew forth from day to day   1 Chron. xvi. His salvation.'   23, 35.

'Stand ye still, and see the salvation of the Lord with you.'   2 Chron. xx. 17.

'Behold, God is my salvation; I will trust, and not be afraid; for   Isa. xii. 2. the Lord Jehovah is my strength and my song,' etc.

Psalm XIV

(*Seven Verses*)   Verse

This is almost word for word the same as the 53rd Psalm (which consists of six verses). The Psalmist, reflecting upon the folly of the man who denies God, declares it is the 'fool' who says in his heart 'There is no God.' From heaven God looks down upon the   2 'children of men' and knows those who 'seek Him,' for 'God is in the generation of the righteous.'

PARALLEL VERSES

'The way of a fool is right in his own eyes.'   Prov. xi. 15-16.

'A fool layeth open his folly.'   Prov. xiii. 16.

'A wise man feareth, and departeth from evil, but the fool rageth   Prov. xiv. 14. and is confident.'

'A foolish son is a grief to his father and a bitterness to her that   Prov. xvii. 25. bare him.'

'A fool hath no delight in understanding.'   Prov. xviii. 2.

Thus has the wise man defined the Psalmist's words of a 'fool.'

Psalm XV

(*Five Verses*)

The Psalmist describes the character of a true man, a worthy citizen of Zion: he 'walketh uprightly'; he does not injure his neighbour by word or deed, neither does he take up a 'reproach' against him, whilst a 'vile' person is contemned in his sight, and he 'honours' those who

fear God ; he does not backbite with his tongue, or injure his neighbour ; he is incapable of a bribe, nor would he 'put his money out
to usury '—he works for righteousness. Such a man can never be
moved.

PARALLEL VERSES

Gen. v. 24.   Enoch walked with God.'

Gen. vi. 9.   'Noah was a just man, and perfect in his generations, and Noah
walked with God.'

Lev. xix. 2.   'Speak unto all the congregation of the children of Israel, and say
unto them, Ye shall be holy; for I the Lord your God am holy.'

Deut. xviii. 13.   'Thou shalt be perfect with the Lord thy God.'

Prov. ii. 21.   'The upright shall dwell in the land, and the perfect shall remain
in it.'

Prov. iv. 23.   'Keep thy heart with all diligence ; for out of it are the issues of
life.'

Zech. viii. 17.   Let none of you imagine evil in your hearts against his neighbour.'

Mal. ii. 16.   'Take heed to your spirit that ye deal not treacherously.'

Psalm XVI

(*Eleven Verses*)

A protest against idolatry. The Psalmist declares that God is the
portion of his inheritance ; 'Yea,' he says, 'I have a goodly heritage.'
In his faith he trusts that God will shew him 'the path of life,' for in
His presence is 'fulness of joy,' and 'pleasures for evermore.'

PARALLEL VERSES

Num. xviii. 18.   'And the Lord spake unto Aaron, Thou shalt have no inheritance in
their land.   I am thy part and thine inheritance among the children of
Israel.'

Ps. xxxiii. 12.   'Blessed is the nation whose God is the Lord ; and the people
whom He hath chosen for His own inheritance.'

Ps. lxxiii. 26.   'God is the strength of my heart, and my portion for ever.'

Lamen. iii. 24.   'The Lord is my portion, saith my soul; therefore will I hope in
Him.'

Psalm XVII

(*Fifteen Verses*)

In this prayer the Psalmist gives full expression to the basis upon which rests his faith in the efficacy of his prayer, viz., the 'integrity of his own heart.' My prayer goeth not out of 'feigned lips'; he prays for Divine inspiration in every 'sentence' that he utters, so that his 'mouth' shall not transgress. It is with confidence that he exclaims, 'Hear my speech.'

1

3

The Psalmist shows in bold contrast the 'men of the world,' whose 'portion' is in 'this life'; they speak 'proudly,' enclosed in their own 'fat,' their 'eyes bowing down to the earth,' deadly enemies to those who look up to God for help and guidance at every step ! 'Hold up my goings in Thy paths, that my footsteps slip not.' 'Keep me as the apple of the eye.' He concludes with this expression of his faith in the future : 'As for me, I will behold Thy face in righteousness : I shall be satisfied, when I awake, with Thy likeness.'

PARALLEL VERSES

'The children of thy people say, The way of the Lord is not equal : but as for them their way is not equal.' — Ezek. xxxiii. 17.

'These six things doth the Lord hate ; yea, seven are an abomination unto Him : a proud look, a lying tongue, hands that shed innocent blood, a heart that deviseth wicked imaginations, feet that be swift in running to mischief, a false witness that speaketh lies, and he that soweth discord among brethren.' — Prov. vi. 16, 17, 18, 19.

. Every one that is proud is an abomination to the Lord.' — Prov. xvi. 5.

' Make Thy way straight before my face.' — Ps. v. 8.

'The work of righteousness shall be peace.' — Isa. xxxii. 17.

' In the way of righteousness is life ; and in the pathway thereof there is no death.' — Prov. xii. 28.

Psalm XVIII

(*Fifty Verses*)

This Psalm is contained in the twenty-second chapter of the Second Book of Samuel (consisting of fifty-one verses). It was written upon the

2 Sam. xxii. 1. occasion of a great victory, and deliverance from the enemy, and from 'out of the hand of Saul.'

Verses

1

  David attributes the glory to God, and to Him alone. He pours out the enthusiasm of his Divine affections in a song of praise. 'I will love Thee, O Lord, my strength.' The Psalmist declares his faith in the infinite power of God to help frail man on earth when in distress, he

4

6

cries to Him. 'The sorrows of death compassed me, and the floods of ungodly men made me afraid. . . . In my distress I called upon the Lord, and cried unto my God : He heard my voice out of His temple and my cry came before Him, even unto His ears.' The purpose of this Psalm is sustained to the last verse, viz., the glory of God and His infinite power to help us. 'Therefore will I give thanks unto Thee, O

49

50

Lord, among the heathen, and sing praises unto Thy name.' 'Great deliverance giveth He to His king ; and sheweth mercy to His anointed, to David, and to his seed for evermore.'

Parallel Verses

1 Kings i. 29. 'And the king sware and said, As the Lord liveth, that hath redeemed my soul out of all distress, even as I sware unto thee by the Lord God of Israel, saying, Assuredly Solomon thy son shall reign after me, and he shall sit upon my throne in my stead ; even so will I certainly do this day.'

1 Kings iii. 3. 'And Solomon loved the Lord, walking in the statutes of David his father.'

1 Kings viii. 23. 'And he (Solomon) said, Lord God of Israel, there is no God like Thee, in heaven above, or on earth beneath, who keepest covenant and mercy with Thy servants that walk before Thee with all their heart.'

1 Kings ix. 3.
1 Kings ix. 4. 'And the Lord said unto him, I have heard thy prayer ; . . . . and if thou wilt walk before me as David thy father walked, in integrity of

1 Kings ix. 5. heart, and in uprightness, . then I will establish the throne of thy kingdom upon Israel for ever, as I promised to David thy father.'

1 Chron. xi. 9. '. . . . David waxed greater and greater ; for the Lord of hosts was with him.'

  This chapter records a Psalm of David commencing thus :

1 Chron. xvi. 7. 'Give thanks unto the Lord, call upon His name.'

1 Chron. xxviii. 9. (David said) 'Thou Solomon, my son, know thou the God of thy

father, and serve Him with a perfect heart and with a willing mind : for
the Lord searcheth all hearts, and understandeth all the imaginations of
the thoughts : if thou seek Him, He will be found of thee. . . . And 1 Chron. xxix.
David said, 'Blessed be Thou, Lord God of Israel our father, for ever 10.
and ever.'

Psalm XIX

(*Fourteen Verses*)

Verses

The Psalmist looks up to the 'firmament': he declares the 'glory
of God' in the 'heavens.'   In contemplating the wondrous sight above,
his mind becomes elevated ; he exclaims, 'Night unto night sheweth
knowledge.'   After describing the rising of the sun in the morning, 2
he reflects upon the perfect laws of God acting upon the life of
Man—'more to be desired than gold,' 'sweeter than honey and the
honeycomb'—because by means of God's laws to man he is 'warned' 10
against temptation ; his eyes become enlightened, so that he may 11
control his 'secret faults.'   Finally, he prays that these reflections may 12
find acceptance in the sight of God.

PARALLEL VERSES

'I will make them hear My words, that they may learn to fear Me Deut. iv. 10.
all the days that they shall live upon the earth, and that they may teach
their children.'

'How sweet are Thy words unto my taste ! yea, sweeter than honey Ps. cxix. 103,
to my mouth !' 104.

'Through Thy precepts I get understanding : therefore I hate every Ps. cxix. 104,
false way.   Thy word is a lamp unto my feet, and a light unto my path.' 105.

'Evil men understand not judgment : but they that seek the Lord Prov. xxviii. 5.
understand all things.'

'Remember ye the law of Moses My servant, which I commanded Malachi iv. 4.
unto him in Horeb for all Israel, with the statutes and judgments.'

Psalm XX

(*Nine Verses*)

Verses

This is a hymn of praise, in which the people bless their king ('God's 6
anointed').   They pray that the 'God of Jacob' may defend him in the 1
'day of trouble,' and that all his heart's wishes may be fulfilled.   'Some

Verse

7

trust in chariots, and some in horses, but we will remember the name of the Lord our God.'

PARALLEL VERSES

Ps. xxxiii. 16, 17.

'There is no king saved by the multitude of a host : a mighty man is not delivered by much strength. An horse is a vain thing for safety · neither shall he deliver any by his great strength.'

Job xxxix. 19.

'Hast thou given the horse strength? Hast thou clothed his neck

Job xxxix. 21.

with thunder?   he   . . rejoiceth in his strength : he goeth on to meet the armed men.'

Psalm XXI

Verses

(*Thirteen Verses*)

In this thanksgiving Psalm the king makes a summary, as it were, of the special blessings bestowed upon him, the reigning king of Israel,

3

with a 'crown of pure gold on his head,' in the possession of both

5

honour and majesty ; but it is not upon these outer signs of God's favour that the king relies. Truly he asked that his life might be

2

spared, and God granted him the 'request of his lips'; but that which the king most prizes is the spiritual life, those blessings that cannot

6

cease with this life, 'for Thou hast made him most blessed for ever.'

7

'For the king trusteth in the Lord, and through the mercy of the Most High he shall not be moved.' He concludes with these words,

13

'Be Thou exalted, Lord, in Thine own strength : so will we sing and praise Thy power.'

PARALLEL VERSES

1 Kings iii. 12, 13.

'Behold, I have done according to thy words : lo I have given thee a wise and an understanding heart. . . . And I have also given thee that which thou hast not asked, both riches and honour.'

1 Chron. xxix. 10.

'David blessed the Lord before all the congregation : and David said, Blessed be Thou, Lord God of Israel our father, for ever and

1 Chron. xxix. 20.

ever.   And all the congregation blessed the Lord God of their fathers, and bowed down their heads, and worshipped the Lord.'

Isa. xii. 2.

'Behold, God is my salvation ; I will trust and not be afraid ; for the Lord Jehovah is my strength and my song, He also is become my

salvation. · · · Trust ye in the Lord for ever : for in the Lord Jehovah Isa. xxvi. 4.
is everlasting strength.'

'Whoso trusteth in the Lord, happy is he.' Prov. xvi. 20.

Psalm XXII

(*Thirty-one Verses*)

\Verses

This Psalm is a prayer and meditation written in a season of great
distress. The Psalmist pours out his soul laden with sorrow that
would be helpless despair but for the remembrance of the faith of his 4, 5
fathers. 'Our fathers trusted in Thee : they trusted, and Thou didst
deliver them. They cried unto Thee, and were delivered : they trusted
in Thee, and were not confounded.'

The Psalmist records the personal cruelties to which he was sub-
jected, but that which more than all afflicted him was the reproach of
the ungodly, who scornfully said, 'He trusted in the Lord, let 8
Him deliver him'—he was brought unto the 'dust of death.' Now 15
he reflects upon God's wonderful care of him from his birth : he 10
exclaims again and again, 'Be not far from me ; for trouble is near ; 11, 19
for there is none to help, ... O Lord : O my strength, haste Thee to
help me.' After these outpourings to God, he declares his faith to his 22
brethren, in the midst of the congregation, and calls upon those of the
seed of Jacob (Israel) who fear God, to praise Him in the 'great 25
congregation, so that 'all the ends of the world' and all the 'kindreds 27
of the nations' shall worship God, for the 'kingdom is the Lord's'
and He is governor among the nations ! A 'seed shall serve Him 30
accounted as a generation.' Your heart shall live for ever.' In conclusion, the Psalmist says that the righteousness of God shall be 31
declared to a 'people that shall be born.'

Parallel Verses

'   The word of our God shall stand for ever.' Isa. xl. 8.

'Look unto Me, and be ye saved, all the ends of the earth : for I Isa. xlv. 22, 25.
am God, and there is none else. . . . In the Lord shall all the seed
of Israel be justified, and shall glory.'

'Behold, the days come, saith the Lord, that I will perform that good Jer. xxxiii. 14,
thing which I have promised unto the house of Israel, and to the house 25.
of Judah. . . . If My covenant be not with day and night, and if I

have not appointed the ordinances of heaven and earth ; then will I cast away the seed of Jacob, and David My servant whose seed shall not be rulers over the seed of Abraham, Isaac, and Jacob.'

Malachi iii. 6.   '   I am the Lord, I change not; therefore ye sons of Jacob are not consumed.'

Psalm XXIII

Verses

(*Six Verses*)

This Psalm describes the peaceful life of the youth David, when, as a shepherd lad, he was minding his father's sheep. Great was his faith in God ; he had not learnt the art of war, but he had already experienced the help of God in extremity, as told by himself. Thus he

3   describes the peace of a spiritual life with God on earth : ' He restoreth

4   my soul : . . . . Yea, though I walk through the valley of the shadow

6   of death, I will fear no evil: for Thou art with me. . . . Surely goodness and mercy shall follow me all the days of my life : I will dwell in the house of the Lord for ever.'

PARALLEL VERSES

1 Sam. xvi.   In the early history of David we read that, when it was Samuel's sacred mission to anoint a king in the place of Saul (then king of

1 Sam. xvi. 10. Israel), Jesse (the father of David) caused seven of his sons to pass

1 Sam. xvi. 11. before Samuel. . . . And Samuel said unto Jesse, Are here all thy children ? And he said, There remaineth yet the youngest, and behold

1 Sam. xvi. 12. he keepeth the sheep. Samuel said to Jesse, Send and fetch him . . . . And he sent and brought him in. Now he was ruddy, and withal of a beautiful countenance, and goodly to look to. And the Lord said,

1 Sam. xvi. 13. Arise, anoint him : for this is he. 'Then Samuel took the horn of oil, and anointed him in the midst of his brethren.'

1 Sam. xvii. 42. When called upon to meet the giant Philistine, he was 'but a youth' :

1 Sam. xvii. 40. he chose him five smooth stones out of the brook, and put them in a

1 Sam. xvii. 45. shepherd's bag which he had. . . . Then said David to the Philistine, Thou comest to me with a 'sword,' 'spear,' and 'shield': but I come to thee in the name of the Lord of hosts, the God of the armies of

1 Sam. xvii. 46. Israel whom thou hast defied, ... that all the earth may know that there is a God in Israel.

Psalm XXIV

(Ten Verses)

This Psalm proclaims the infinite power of God in the world. By the development of our spiritual life with God the soul becomes reunited with God in love (divine and human), and recognises the 'everlasting doors,' and shall receive the 'blessing from the Lord, and righteousness from the God of his salvation.'

5

Parallel Verses

' He is the Lord our God ; His judgments are in all the earth, the word that He commanded to a thousand generations.'

1 Chron. xvi. 14, 15.

'God is in the generation of the righteous.'

Ps. xiv. 5.

'Thou, O Lord, remainest for ever.'

Lam. v. 19.

Psalm XXV

(Twenty-two Verses)

In this Psalm the supplicant pours out his faith in God ; he prays for divine guidance in every step of life ; his belief in forgiveness of sin rests upon his conception of God's infinite love. 'The meek will He guide in judgment : and the meek will He teach His way.'

9

The paths of the Lord are mercy and truth. . . . The 'secret' of the Lord is with those whose eyes are continually towards Him in sacred communion. In times of trouble and affliction he prays, 'O bring Thou me out of my distresses ;   . for I put my trust in Thee.'

10
17
20

Parallel Verses

'Now the man Moses was very meek above all the men which were upon the face of the earth. . . . With him will I speak, mouth to mouth, even apparently, and not in dark speeches.'

Num. xii. 3.
Num. xii. 8.

'Seek ye the Lord, all ye meek of the earth, which have wrought His judgment ; seek righteousness, seek meekness.'

Zeph. ii. 3.

'Thus saith the high and lofty One, that inhabiteth eternity, whose name is Holy ; I dwell in the high and holy place, with him also that is of a contrite and humble spirit, to revive the spirit of the humble, and to revive the heart of the contrite ones.'

Isa. lvii. 15.

Prov. xxix. 23.   'A man's pride shall bring him low : but honour shall uphold the humble in spirit.'

Psalm XXVI

Verses

(Twelve Verses)

The Psalmist finds comfort in a brief contemplation of his past life ; he is sustained in the consciousness of his own integrity ; he calls to mind the many occasions on which he has resisted temptation—how he had refused to follow the multitude in their wickedness and evil habits, he has refused to sit with dissemblers or vain persons, but his delight has been in the house of God, because he trusted in Him. In the con-

2   sciousness of his own innocence he fearlessly exclaims, 'Examine me O God, and prove me : try my reins and my heart.'

12   '   In the congregation will I bless the Lord.'

PARALLEL VERSES

Gen. xx. 5.   '   In the integrity of my heart and innocency of my hands have

Gen. xx. 6.   I done this. And God said unto him in a dream, Yea, I know that thou didst this in the integrity of thy heart.'

Job xxvii. 3.   Job said, ... 'While my breath is in me, and the spirit of God is

Job xxvii. 4.   in my nostrils, my lips shall not speak wickedness, nor my tongue utter

Job xxvii. 5.   deceit ; .   till I die I will not remove mine integrity from me ;

Job xxvii. 6.   . . . . my heart shall not reproach me so long as I live.'

Prov. xix. 1.   ' Better is the poor that walketh in his integrity, than he that is perverse in his lips, and is a fool.'

Psalm XXVII

Verses

Fourteen Verses

By his great faith in God the Psalmist rises to a spiritual height, beyond which it is not possible to ascend whilst clothed in mortal life. By his moral courage he is fearless, though surrounded by those who are

12   'false witnesses' and 'such as breathe out cruelty'; but he believed in

13   the 'goodness of God' in the 'land of the living.'

14   He says, 'Wait on the Lord : be of good courage, and He shall strengthen thine heart.'

'The name of the Lord is a strong tower : the righteous runneth into Prov. xix. 10. it, and is safe.'

'The Lord God is my strength, ... and He will make my feet like Hab. iii. 19. hinds' feet.'

'Ye shall be a blessing : fear not, but let your hands be strong.' Zech. viii. 13.

'I will strengthen them in the Lord, and they shall walk up and Zech. x. 12. down in His name, saith the Lord.'

Psalm XXVIII

(*Nine Verses*)

Verses

This is one of those outpourings of the soul in which the Psalmist feels keenly that unless God has heard his prayer he becomes like them that 'go down into the pit,' for his surroundings are 'workers 1 of iniquity,' who speak 'peace to their neighbours' whilst 'mischief is in their hearts.' In the consciousness that God has heard the voice 3 of his supplication his mind becomes calm and joyful, and he is 'helped.'

PARALLEL VERSES

'Behold, I am the Lord, the God of all flesh : is there anything too Jer. xxxii. 27. hard for Me?'

'The prayer of the upright is His delight.' Prov. xv. 8.

'Then shall ye call upon Me, and ye shall go and pray unto Me, and Jer. xxix. 12. I will hearken unto you ; and ye shall seek Me, and find Me when ye Jer. xxix. 13. shall search for Me with all your heart.'

Psalm XXIX

(*Eleven Verses*)

Verse

This is a hymn of glory. Men of power are called to worship God 2 'in the beauty of holiness.' The voice of God is upon the waters and the dry land, and resounds through the wilderness as through the forest. God reigns as King for ever. There is a beautiful transition of thought from the majesty to the tenderness of God : 'The Lord will give strength unto His people ; the Lord will bless His people with peace.'

PARALLEL VERSES

Zeph. iii. 14.   'Sing, O daughter of Zion ; shout, O Israel ; be glad and rejoice with all the heart, O daughter of Jerusalem '

Haggai ii. 5.   'According to the word that I covenanted with you, when ye came out of Egypt, so My spirit remaineth among you : fear ye not.'

Joel ii. 21.   'Fear not, O land ; be glad and rejoice ; for the Lord will do great

Joel ii. 27.   things, and ye shall know that I am in the midst of Israel, and that I am the Lord your God, and none else : and My people shall never be ashamed.'

Psalm XXX

(Twelve Verses)

Verses

The Psalmist contemplates the triumph of joy over sorrow. 'Weep-

5   ing may endure for a night, but joy cometh in the morning.'   In life we must sing praises to God ; for quick is often the transition from mourn-

12   ing to gladness. '. . . O Lord my God, I will give thanks unto Thee for ever and ever.'

PARALLEL VERSES

1 Chron. xxix.
10.   'David blessed the Lord before all the congregation : and David said, Blessed be Thou, Lord God of Israel our father, for ever and ever.'

Neh. ix. 5.   'Stand up and bless the Lord your God for ever and ever : and blessed be Thy glorious name, which is exalted above all blessing and praise.'

Jer. xxxii. 18.   '   The great, the mighty God, the Lord of hosts, is His name.'

Psalm XXXI

(Twenty-four Verses)

\erses

This soul-stirring Psalm gives expression to the highest form of spiritual worship and knowledge of God.   The Psalmist communes with God in such nearness that he can say, 'Thou hast considered my

7   trouble ; Thou hast known my soul in adversities.' 'Bow down Thine ear to me' ; 'in Thee do I put my trust.' 'I trusted in Thee, O

15   Lord : I said, Thou art my God.   My times are in Thy hand.'   He

pours out his heart as he could do to no human being, the result being that his courage revives ; he exclaims, ' Oh, how great is Thy goodness, which Thou hast laid up for them that fear Thee, which Thou hast wrought for them that trust in Thee, before the sons of men ! '

PARALLEL VERSES

(When Moses said to God) ' I beseech Thee, shew me Thy glory' Exod. xxxiii. 18.
(the reply follows) : 'And He said, I will make all My goodness Exod. xxxiv. 19.
pass before Thee, and I will proclaim the name of the Lord before Thee : and I will be gracious to whom I will be gracious, and will shew mercy on whom I will shew mercy.'

' And the Lord passed by before him, and proclaimed, The Lord, Exod. xxxiv. 6.
the Lord God, merciful and gracious, longsuffering, and abundant in goodness and truth.'

(Moses addresses the people) ' If thou shalt seek the Lord thy God, Deut. iv. 29.
thou shalt find Him, if thou seek Him with all thy heart, and with all thy soul ;   (for the Lord thy God is a merciful God).' Deut. iv. 31.

Psalm XXXII
(*Eleven Verses*)

This Psalm is perhaps one of the most important in the whole collection, because it contains a theory affecting the lives of many in every generation.   It speaks of an invisible line drawn between ' iniquity' and 'sin,' though the terms are synonymous.   'Sin' may be described as a violation of the law of God, or neglect of known duty, whilst 'iniquity' (though also 'sin') is described as wickedness or crime.   A 'sin' may have been committed under conditions of helplessness or temptation, the 'iniquity' of that 'sin' may be forgiven by means of prayer and repentance, of which God alone is the judge. Confession of transgression is not necessarily penitence.   The man or woman 'in whose spirit there is no guile' is known to God.   The over whelmings of sorrow for transgressions, and the joy of the upright, whose ' iniquity' is forgiven, are described in this Psalm.

PARALLEL VERSES

'   He said to the judges, Take heed what ye do, for ye 2 Chron. 6.
judge not for man, but for the Lord, who is with you in judgment.'

2 Chron. xix. 7.

'. . . . Let the fear of the Lord be upon you : take heed and do it : for there is no iniquity with the Lord our God, nor respect of persons, nor taking of gifts.'

2 Chron. xix. 9.

'Thus shall ye do in the fear of the Lord, faithfully, and with a perfect heart.'

Ps. xxxii. 5, 6.

NOTE.—Parallel verses which treat of 'iniquity' and 'sin' are too numerous for entry here. The Psalmist exclaimed : 'Thou forgavest the iniquity of my sin. For this shall every one pray unto Thee in a time when Thou mayest be found.'

Mal. iii. 7.

'Return unto Me, and I will return unto you, saith the Lord of hosts.'

Psalm XXXIII
(*Twenty-two Verses*)

\erses

This joyous Psalm of praise is an unbroken discourse on the providence of God in His relations with man on earth. 'The Lord

13 looketh from heaven.' 'He looketh upon all the inhabitants of the

14 earth.' Our 'hearts shall rejoice in Him,' because He is infinite in

5 goodness, righteousness, and power. He loves righteousness. The 'earth is full of the goodness of the Lord.' 'Blessed is the nation

12 whose God is the Lord, and the people whom He hath chosen for His

20, 22 own inheritance.' 'He is our help and our shield.' 'Let Thy mercy be upon us, according as we hope in Thee.'

PARALLEL VERSES

Deut. xxxii. 9.
Deut. xxxii. 10.

'The Lord's portion is His people : Jacob is the lot of His inheritance. . . . He kept him as the apple of His eye.'

Deut. xxxii. 27.

'The eternal God is thy refuge.'

Deut. xxxii. 29.

'Happy art thou, O Israel : who is like unto thee, O people saved by the Lord, the Shield of thy help ?'

2 Chron. xvi. 9.

'The eyes of the Lord run to and fro throughout the whole earth to shew Himself strong in behalf of them whose heart is perfect towards Him.'

Jer. xvi. 17.

'Mine eyes are upon all their ways.'

Job xxxiv. 21.

'His eyes are upon the ways of man, and He seeth all his goings.'

Prov. xv. 3.

'The eyes of the Lord are in every place, beholding the evil and the good.'

'Thou art of purer eyes than to behold evil, and canst not look on   Hab. i. 13.
iniquity.'

The 'eyes of the Lord, which run to and fro through the whole   Zech. iv. 10.
earth.'

Psalm XXXIV

(*Twenty-two Verses*)

\erses

This Psalm is absolutely full of hope; the result of the soul's
victory over every depressing condition of mortal life. The Psalmist
tells the personal experiences of his life with God in the world. 'My
soul shall make her boast in the Lord; the humble shall hear it   2
and be glad.' 'I sought the Lord, and He heard me, and delivered   4
me from all my fears.' Those who look up to God are enlightened and
never ashamed. The 'poor man' cried to God, and was delivered   6
from all his troubles; for those who seek God shall 'not want any good 10
thing.' He tells the young to 'keep their tongues from evil,' from
'speaking guile,' to 'seek peace' and to 'do good,' for 'the eyes of the 15
Lord are upon the righteous, and His ears are open unto their cry'; that
God is near to the 'broken-hearted,' and although the righteous have   18
many afflictions, God can deliver them out of all.

Parallel Verses

'The Lord maketh poor and maketh rich. He bringeth low and   1 Sam. ii. 7.
lifteth up. He raiseth up the poor out of the dust, and lifteth up the   1 Sam. ii. 8.
beggar from the dunghill, to set them among princes, and to make
them inherit the throne of glory; for the pillars of the earth are the
Lord's, and He has set the world upon them.'

'Acquaint now thyself with Him, and be at peace; thereby good shall   Job xvii. 21.
come unto thee. . . . For then shalt thou have thy delight in the   Job xxii. 26.
Almighty.'

'The rich and poor meet together; the Lord is the maker of them   Prov. xxii. 2
all.'

'For Thou hast been a strength to the poor, a strength to the needy   Isa. xxv. 4.
in his distress, a refuge from the storm, a shadow from the heat.'

Psalm XXXV

(*Twenty-eight Verses*)

Verses

This whole Psalm has been written under exceptional conditions of exasperation, such as are not within the ordinary experiences of our daily

7   life. The Psalmist is persecuted without a cause, he is exposed to the
16   sport of 'hypocritical mockers,' whereas 'when they were sick' he
21   prayed for them, and behaved like a friend 'or brother—'as one
14   mourneth for his mother.' His indignation is human, but he rises in
his faith to the balancing influences of his spiritual nature, and finds comfort. 'O Lord, be not far from me, and my tongue shall speak of
22   Thy righteousness, and of Thy praise all the day long.'

Parallel Verses

Jer. xv. 17.   'I sat not in the assembly of the mockers nor rejoiced; I sat alone because of Thy hand : for Thou hast filled me with indignation.'

Jer. xv. 20, 21.   'I am with thee to save thee and to deliver thee, saith the Lord. 'And I will deliver thee out of the hand of the wicked, and I will redeem thee out of the hand of the terrible.'

Job v. 8.   'I would seek unto God, and unto God would I commit my cause.'

Job xxiii. 6.   'Will He plead against me with His great power? No ; but He would put strength in me.'

Prov. xx. 22.   'Say not thou, I will recompense evil; but wait on the Lord, and He shall save thee.'

Psalm XXXVI

(*Twelve Verses*)

Verses

The Psalmist meditates on the wickedness of man : his sins are the

2   result of 'flattering himself in his own eyes,' until his iniquity becomes
3   hateful ; his words are 'iniquity and deceit,' he 'deviseth mischief upon
7   his bed,' he 'abhorreth not evil.' He contrasts the lovingkindness
9   of God—'for with Thee is the fountain of life : in Thy light shall
11   we see light.' Finally he prays for the continuance of God's loving-kindness, and that the 'foot of pride come not against him.'

'The fear of the Lord is to hate evil: pride, and arrogancy, and the Prov. viii. 13.
evil way, and the froward mouth do I hate.'

'I will punish the world for their evil, and the wicked for their Isa. xiii. 11.
iniquity; and I will cause the arrogancy of the proud to cease, and
will lay low the haughtiness of the terrible.'

'The pride of thine heart hath deceived thee, .   that saith in his Oba. i. 3.
heart, Who shall bring me down to the ground?'

Psalm XXXVII
(*Forty Verses*)
Verses

This Psalm consists of a series of exhortations, appealing to man in
his varied experiences. Many there are who waste their lives, in a
rebellious spirit, against the inequalities of life, to whom the Psalmist
says, 'A little that a righteous man hath is better than the riches of   16
many wicked.'

It is specially directed against vexation of spirit. The Psalmist
reflects upon his personal experiences. 'I have been young and now   5
am old, yet have I not seen the righteous forsaken.' 'I have seen   35
the wicked in great power, and spreading himself like a green bay
tree: yet he passed away; . . . . I sought him, but he could not be
found.' 'The Lord knoweth the days of the upright; and their inheritance shall be for ever.' The end of that man is peace.   37

'Wrath killeth the foolish man, and envy slayeth the silly one.'   Job v. 2.

'Wherefore do the wicked live, become old, yea, are mighty in Job xxi. 7.
power?   . They spend their days in wealth, and in a moment go Job xxi. 13.
down to the grave. Therefore they say unto God, Depart from us; for Job xxi. 14.
we desire not the knowledge of Thy ways.'

'He that is soon angry dealeth foolishly.'   Prov. xiv. 17.

'He that is slow to anger is better than the mighty; and he that Prov. xvi. 32.
ruleth his spirit than he that taketh a city.'

Prov. xxv. 28.   'He that has no rule over his own spirit is like a city that is broken down, and without walls.'

Prov. xxix. 23.   'A man's pride shall bring him low; but honour shall uphold the humble in spirit.'

Psalm XXXVIII
(*Twenty-two Verses*)

Verses

The first thirteen verses of this Psalm describe the condition of a man whose sufferings, both physical and mental, are so terrible that the bare record of them must strike every heart with compassion. He is

8

'sore broken,' 'feeble,' and disquieted; his words fail him, like a

13

man both deaf and dumb. What, then, upheld him? It was his

15

inward silent faith in God. 'For in Thee, O Lord, do I hope: Thou

17

wilt hear, O Lord my God.' Again he refers to his sorrows, and he

18

declares his repentance for sin, and clings to God. 'Forsake me not,

21, 22

O God: O my God, be not far from me; make haste to help me, O Lord my salvation.'

PARALLEL VERSES

Job x. 1.   'My soul is weary of my life: I will leave my complaint upon myself: I will speak in the bitterness of my soul.'

Job xvi. 20.   'My friends scorn me: but mine eye poureth out tears unto God.'

Isa. xxxviii. 14.   '   I did mourn as a dove: mine eyes fail with looking upward: O Lord, I am oppressed; undertake for me.'

Isa. xxxviii. 17.   'Behold, for peace I had great bitterness: but Thou hast in love to my soul delivered it from the pit of corruption: for Thou hast cast all my sins behind my back.'

Psalm XXXIX
(*Thirteen Verses*)

Verses

The Psalmist reflects upon the philosophy of human life—its vani-

12

ties, its brevity. He says, I am a 'stranger,' 'a sojourner, as all my

6

fathers were.' Man walks in a 'vain shew'; he heaps up riches, and knows not who shall gather them. The Psalmist prays to know the measure of his days, 'what it is; that I may know how frail I am.'

13

'O spare me, that I may recover strength before I go hence and be no more.'

PARALLEL VERSES

'   The righteous hath hope in his death.'   Prov. xiv. 32.

'Righteousness exalteth a nation : but sin is a reproach to any Prov. xiv. 34.
people.'

'The work of righteousness shall be peace, and the effect of Isa. xxxii. 17.
righteousness, quietness, and assurance for ever.'

Psalm XL

(Seventeen Verses)   Verses

The Psalmist takes a retrospective view of his life; he has
preached to the 'great congregation' that which he knew to be God's   10
truth ; he has not hidden within his own heart the righteousness and
lovingkindness of God.   His delight was to do the will of God, for
he felt that the 'law of God' was 'within his heart.'   Hence he would   8
not 'refrain' his 'lips'; he declared that God desired neither sacrifice   9
nor offering for sin.   He looks back upon the miseries of his past life,   6
when his enemies taunted him ; but he 'waited for the Lord,' and   15
God heard his cry; so now he sings a 'new song,' even 'praise unto   1
our God.'

PARALLEL VERSES

'The Lord will not suffer the soul of the righteous to famish.'   Prov. x. 3.

'To do justice and judgment is more acceptable to the Lord than Prov. xxi. 3.
sacrifice.'

'Though ye offer me burnt offerings, and your meat offerings, I will Amos v. 22,
not accept them. . . . But let judgment run down as waters, and   24.
righteousness as a mighty stream.'

'The way of the just is uprightness.   Thou, most upright, dost Isa. xxvi. 7.
weigh the path of the just.'

'When Thy judgments are in the earth, the inhabitants of the world Isa. xxvi. 9.
will learn righteousness.'

Psalm XLI

(Thirteen Verses)

The Psalmist reflects upon the blessing to those who have considered the poor ; he believes that in the time of their sickness God

3   will 'strengthen them upon the bed of languishing.' He complains bitterly that in his illness he is visited by his enemies, who whisper

7, 8   together against him : 'an evil disease,' say they, cleaveth fast unto

5   him : and now that he lieth he shall rise up no more. His enemies

9   say, 'When shall he die and his name perish?' Even his own familiar friend in whom he trusted is against him. These are sore trials, but he

10   finds comfort in prayer : 'Be merciful unto me and raise me up. . . .

12, 13   Thou upholdest me in mine integrity. Blessed be the Lord God of Israel from everlasting to everlasting. Amen and amen.'

PARALLEL VERSES

Job xxx. 9, 25.   '.   Now am I their song, yea, I am their byword.   Did not I weep for him that was in trouble? Was not my soul grieved for the poor?'

Isa. xxv. 1.   'O Lord, Thou art my God.'

Isa. xxv. 4.   'Thou hast been a strength to the poor, a strength to the needy in his distress, a refuge from the storm, and a shadow from the heat.'

Isa. xli. 10.   'Fear thou not, for I am with thee.'

Isa. xli. 13.   'I, the Lord thy God, will hold thy right hand, saying unto thee, Fear not ; I will help thee.'

Psalm XLII

(*Eleven Verses*)

1   This Psalm has a special interest because of the simile between the 'hart's' panting after the water brooks and the soul's panting after God—so does the soul 'thirst for God, the living God.' The Psalmist feels keenly that his enemies should tauntingly ask the question, 'Where

10   is thy God?' These words are like a 'sword in my bones'; but when he

5   asks himself, 'Why art thou cast down, O my soul? Why art thou disquieted within me?' the answer comes with an echo that resounds in

8   his soul, and he prays to the 'God of his life.' He asks himself, why

9   should he go mourning because of the oppression of the enemy, who has not known the comforting influence of the divine countenance that beams with infinite love and sympathy? How great is the joyous hope !

'I shall yet praise God for the help of His countenance.' That divine 'help' is oftentimes seen as through a glass, reflecting within ourselves. The Psalmist says, 'Hope thou in God, for I shall yet praise Him, who is the health of my countenance, and my God.'

PARALLEL VERSES

The 'hart' is mentioned as among the list of 'clean' food that 'may be eaten.'   Deut. xii 15.

The Preacher, describing the future glory of Israel, when all that is now wrong shall be made right, says, 'Then shall the lame man leap as an hart,' the 'dumb sing.'   'Strengthen ye the weak hands ; . . . . say to them that are of a fearful heart, Be strong, fear not. . . . This shall be called The way of holiness.'   Isa. xxxv. 6. Isa. xxxv. 3. Isa. xxxv. 8.

'The way of the just is uprightness.   With my soul have I desired Thee in the night ; yea, with my spirit within me will I seek Thee early.'   Isa. xxvi. 7, 9.

'The Lord is my portion, saith my soul ; therefore will I hope in Him.'   Lam. iii. 24.

Psalm XLIII
(*Five Verses*)

In these few verses, the Psalmist soars to an exalted spiritual faith possible to life on earth with God.   'Thou art the God of my strength.

O send out Thy light and Thy truth ; let them lead me, ... God, my exceeding joy.   Yea, upon the harp will I praise Thee, O God, my God.'

He repeats the last words of the previous Psalm : '. . . . I shall yet praise Him, who is the health of my countenance, and my God.'

PARALLEL VERSES

'   Ascribe ye greatness unto our God.   He is the Rock, His work is perfect : for all His ways are judgment : a God of truth and without iniquity, just and right is He.'   Deut. xxxii. 3

'Glory ye in His holy name ; let the heart of them rejoice that seek the Lord.   1 Chron xvi. 10.

'Seek the Lord and His strength ; seek His face continually.'   1 Chron. xvi. 11.

1 Chron. xvi.
14.   'He is the Lord our God.'

29.   '   Worship the Lord in the beauty of holiness.'

Isa. xxx. 18.   'The Lord is a God of judgment : blessed are all they that wait for Him.'

Psalm XLIV

Verses   *(Twenty-six Verses)*

This Psalm is of much later date than the previous ones. The Psalmist refers to incidents of persecution, cruelty, and oppression

14   during Israel's captivity : 'Thou makest us a byword among the
17   heathen, a shaking of the head among the people.' 'All this has come upon us ; yet have we not forgotten Thee, neither have we dealt falsely
19   in Thy covenant,' . . . . though Thou hast 'covered us with the shadow
20   of death. If we have forgotten the name of our God, or stretched out
21   our hand to a strange God ; shall not God search this out? for He knoweth the secrets of the heart.' The Psalmist comforts himself with
1   a retrospect of Israel's history : 'O God, our fathers have told us what
3   work Thou didst in their days, in the times of old. . . . They got not the land in possession ' by their own sword, but through 'the light of
8   God's countenance.' Therefore it is that 'in God we boast all the
26   day long, and praise Thy name for ever.' He prays in these words ·
'Arise for our help, and redeem us for Thy mercies' sake.'

PARALLEL VERSES

Deut. i. 1.   'These be the words which Moses spake unto all Israel ' .

Deut. i. 8.   ' Behold, I have set the land before you ; go in and possess the land, which the Lord sware unto your fathers Abraham, Isaac, and Jacob, to give unto them, and to their seed after them.'

Deut. xxx. 2-5.   'Thou shalt return unto the Lord thy God, and shalt obey His voice ; . . . . then the Lord thy God will turn thy captivity, ... and gather thee from all the nations whither the Lord thy God hath
Deut. xxx. 10.   scattered thee, ... if thou turn unto the Lord thy God with all thine
Deut. xxx. 14.   heart, and with all thy soul. . The word (of God) is very nigh unto thee, in thy mouth, and in thy heart, that thou mayest do it.'

Isa. xlv. 19.   'I have not spoken in secret, in a dark place of the earth : I said not unto the seed of Jacob, seek ye Me in vain : I the Lord speak righteousness, I declare things that are right.'

Psalm XLV

(Seventeen Verses)

This is a song in reference to the reign of King Solomon.   1

God hath 'blessed thee for ever. . . . Instead of thy fathers shall be   2, 16

thy children. . . . I will make thy name to be remembered in all   17

generations. The Psalmist describes the 'Queen in gold of Ophir,   9

. the daughter of Tyre. . . .' The King's daughter 'is all   12, 13

glorious within : her clothing is of wrought gold. . . . She shall be

brought unto the King in raiment of needlework,' with 'gladness and   14

rejoicing' they shall enter the 'King's palace, . . . because of truth,   15

and meekness, and righteousness. . . . Thou lovest righteousness, and   4, 7

hatest wickedness : therefore God, thy God, hath anointed thee with

the oil of gladness.'

PARALLEL VERSES

'And when the Queen of Sheba heard of the fame of Solomon con-   1 Kings x. 1.

cerning the name of the Lord, she came to prove him with hard

questions. .' (She said to him) 'Blessed be the Lord thy God, which   1 Kings x. 7, 8

delighted in thee, to set thee on the throne of Israel : because the Lord   9.

loved Israel for ever, therefore made He thee king, to do judgment

and justice.'

'So King Solomon exceeded all the kings of the earth for riches   1 Kings x. 23.

and for wisdom.'

The prophet, referring to the 'gold of Ophir,' says : 'I will   Isa. xiii. 11, 12.

cause the arrogancy of the proud to cease. . . . I will make a man

more precious than fine gold : even a man than the golden wedge of

Ophir.'

Psalm XLVI

(Eleven Verses)

This Psalm is an outpouring of Israel's faith in God, as a refuge

'and a strength,' and a 'very present help in trouble ;' therefore, though   2, 3, 7

Verse
11

the 'waters roar' and the mountains shake, 'the Lord of hosts is with us ; the God of Jacob is our refuge.'

PARALLEL VERSES

Ex. xv. 2.

'The Lord is my strength and song, and He is become my salvation.

Ex. v. 11.

'He is my God. . . . my father's God.   Who is like unto Thee, O Lord, among the gods ?   Who is like Thee, glorious in holiness, fearful in praises, doing wonders ? '

2 Sam. xxii. 2.
2 Sam. xxii. 3.

'And he (David) said : The Lord is my rock, and my fortress, and my deliverer.   The God of my rock ; in Him will I trust.'

Prov. xiv. 26.

'In the fear of the Lord is strong confidence.'

Prov. xviii. 10.

'The name of the Lord is a strong tower : the righteous runneth into it, and is safe.'

Isa. xii. 2.

'The Lord Jehovah is my strength and my song.'

Isa. xxvi. 4.

'Trust ye in the Lord for ever : for in the Lord Jehovah is everlasting strength.'

Psalm XLVII

Verses

(*Nine Verses*)

This is one of those joyous hymns of praise which appeal to all who worship God in spirit and in truth.

'Sing praise to God, sing praises.'

'For God is the King of all the earth : sing ye praises with understanding.'

PARALLEL VERSES

Ex. xviii. 9.

'And Jethro rejoiced for all the goodness which the Lord had done to Israel. . . . And ye shall rejoice in all that ye put your hand unto, wherein the Lord thy God hath blessed thee. . . .'

Deut. xvi. 11.

'And thou shalt rejoice before the Lord thy God, thou, thy son, and thy daughter. . . .'

1 Chron. xxix. 9.

'Then the people rejoiced, and David the king also rejoiced with great joy. . . .'

2 Chron. xxix. 30.

'. . . . Hezekiah the king and the princes commanded the Levites to sing praise unto the Lord with the words of David. .   And they sang praises with gladness, and they bowed their heads and worshipped.'

1 Sam. ii. 1.

'Hannah prayed and said, My heart rejoiceth in the Lord.'

Psalm XLVIII

(Fourteen Verses)

Another hymn of praise, having reference chiefly to the holy city on Mount Zion where Israel worshipped God in the Temple, and thought of the lovingkindness of God. 'Beautiful for situation, the joy of the whole earth, is Mount Zion, the city of the great King.' 'God is known in her palaces for a refuge. . . . Consider her palaces ; that ye may tell it to the generation following.' 'For this God is our God for ever and ever ;' He will be our guide even beyond death. The common version : 'even unto death.'

Verse

9

2

3, 13

14

PARALLEL VERSES

Joel addressed his people in Jerusalem about 800 years before the present era. He refers to Zion in the following verses : To the inhabitants of the land. Tell your children, and let their children tell another generation concerning the hóly land, and what shall happen, through the sins of the people ; but through repentance and holiness of life with God, the day of rejoicing must come again to the people to whom it belongs. Sanctify ye a fast, call a solemn assembly. . . . O Lord God, to Thee will I cry.

Joel i. 2, 3.

Joel i. 14–19.

'Blow ye the trumpet in Zion, and sound an alarm in My holy mountain : let all the inhabitants of the land tremble : for the day of the Lord cometh, for it is nigh at hand.' After a graphic description of the horrors of warfare, the prophet says, 'He is strong that executeth his word.   Therefore saith the Lord, Turn ye even to Me with all your heart, and with fasting, and with weeping, and with mourning ; and rend your heart, and not your garments, and turn unto the Lord your God : for He is gracious and merciful, slow to anger, and of great kindness, and repenteth Him of the evil.' . . . Then will the Lord be jealous for His land, and pity His people. Yea, the Lord will answer, and say unto His people . . . I will no more make you a reproach among the heathen.   Fear not, O land ; be glad and rejoice : for the Lord will do great things. . . . Be glad then, ye children of Zion, and rejoice in the Lord your God. . . . ye shall praise the name of the Lord your God, that hath dealt wondrously with you : and My people

Joel ii. 1.

Joel ii. 11, 12.

Joel ii. 18.
Joel ii. 19.

Joel ii.
Joel ii. 23
Joel ii. 26.

Joel ii. 27.   shall never be ashamed. And ye shall know that I am in the midst of
Israel, and that I am the Lord your God, and none else : and My
Joel ii. 32.   people shall never be ashamed. .   For in mount Zion and Jerusalem
shall be deliverance, as the Lord hath said.'

Psalm XLIX

Verses   *(Twenty Verses)*

ⲁ   This is an exhortation addressed to all people—'all ye inhabitants of
2   the world : both low and high, rich and poor, together.' It is a fine
17   reflection upon life and death. The Psalmist describes the worldly
12   man, who, although he may win vain applause, 'abideth not';
20   without wisdom, he is 'like the beasts that perish.' The Psalmist
15   reflects upon death when he exclaims : ' But God will redeem my soul
from the power of the grave : for He shall receive me.'

PARALLEL VERSES

Gen. xxvii. 1, 2.   (When Isaac was old, he said to his son :) 'I am old, I know not
the day of my death.'

Deut. xxxii. 29.   'O that they were wise, that they understood this, that they would
consider their latter end !'

1 Chron. xxix.   '. . . . Our days on earth are as a shadow, and there is none
15.   abiding.'

Job vii. 1.   'Is there not an appointed time to man upon earth? are not his
days also like the days of an hireling ?'

Job xxi. 23.   'One dieth in his full strength, being wholly at ease and quiet ; . . . .
Job xxi. 25.   and another dieth in the bitterness of his soul, and never eateth with
Job xxi. 26.   pleasure. They shall lie down alike in the dust.'

Isa. xl. 6.   '. . . . All flesh is grass, and all the goodliness thereof is as the
Isa. lxiv. 6.   flower of the field, ... and we all do fade as a leaf.'

Amos iv. 12.   '   Prepare to meet thy God, O Israel.'

Eccles. ix. 5.   ' For the living know that they shall die.'

Psalm L

(Twenty-three Verses)

This is a homily in which men are rebuked for offering ceremonial sacrifices to God rather than amending their lives. God demands righteousness, and will not accept sacrifices as a substitute. God is not to be deceived by such a system of worship: '. . . . Hear, O My people, and I will speak ; . . . . I am God, even thy God I will not reprove thee for thy sacrifices, or thy burnt offerings, to   8
have been continually before Me.   Every beast of the forest   10
is mine, and the cattle upon a thousand hills ; . . for the world   12
is mine, and the fulness thereof.   . Offer unto God thanksgiving,   14
and pay thy vows unto the Most High : and call upon Me in the day   15
of trouble : I will deliver thee, and thou shalt glorify Me. . . . Thou   21
thoughtest that I was altogether such a one as thyself : but I will
reprove thee.' 'The heavens shall declare his righteousness : for God   6
is judge Himself.' 'Thou sittest and speakest against thy brother ;   20
thou slanderest thine own mother's son.' The Psalmist concludes with
the words : '. . . . To him that ordereth his conversation aright will   23
I shew the salvation of God.'

PARALLEL VERSES

'To what purpose is the multitude of your sacrifices unto Me ?   Isa. i. 11.
saith the Lord : I am full of the burnt offerings of rams.   . I delight
not in the blood of bullocks, or of lambs. . . . When ye come to   Isa. i. 12.
appear before Me, who hath required this at your hand ? . . . . Bring   Isa. i. 13
no more vain oblations : incense is an abomination unto Me ;   Isa. i. 16, 17.
cease to do evil ; learn to do well ; seek judgment, relieve the oppressed,
judge the fatherless, plead for the widow.'

'O my people, they which lead thee cause thee to err, and destroy   Isa. iii. 12.
the way of thy paths.'

'   He that sacrificeth a lamb is as if he cut off a dog's neck ;   Isa. lxvi. 3.
he that offereth an oblation, as if he offered swine's blood ; he that
burneth incense, as if he blessed an idol.'

1 Sam. xv. 22. And Samuel said, Hath the Lord as great delight in burnt offerings and sacrifices, as in obeying the voice of the Lord? Behold, to obey is better than sacrifice, and to hearken than the fat of rams.'

Psalm LI

Verses

(*Nineteen Verses*)

1   The Psalmist, deeply moved by a sense of his own sins, seeks God's mercy 'according to His lovingkindness,' according to the 'multitude of God's tender mercies,' by means of which alone he hopes that his transgressions shall be blotted out. After a full confession of

3, 16   his 'sin' and 'transgressions,' which are ever before him, he says, 'Thou

17   desirest not sacrifice, else would I give it. . . . The sacrifices of God are a broken spirit : a broken and a contrite heart, O God, Thou wilt not despise.' As in the preceding Psalm (l. 2) he thinks of Zion, the 'per-

18   fection of beauty,' where 'God hath shined,' and he prays that in God's 'good pleasure' the 'walls of Jerusalem' shall be restored. The

10-13   Psalmist prays from the depths of his soul for a 'clean heart,' a 'right spirit,' and a fuller sense of the Divine presence. 'Take not Thy

7   holy Spirit from me.' 'Purge me with hyssop, and I shall be clean ·

8   wash me, and I shall be whiter than snow.' He will rejoice and

12, 13   be glad. 'Uphold me with Thy free spirit.' Then will he teach transgressors the ways of God, and sinners shall be converted.

Parallel Verses

Isa. i. 16.   'Wash you, make you clean : put away the evil of your doings from before mine eyes ; cease to do evil. . . .'

Isa. i. 18.   '. . . . Though your sins be as scarlet, they shall be as white as snow   '

2 Chron. vii. 14.   'If My people . . . . shall humble themselves, and pray, and seek My face, and turn from their wicked ways ; then I will hear from heaven, and will forgive their sin   '

2 Chron. xxxiv. 27.   'Because thine heart was tender, and thou didst humble thyself before God . . . . and weep before Me : I have even heard thee also, saith the Lord.'

'Thou art a God ready to pardon, gracious and merciful, slow to Neh. ix. 17.
anger, and of great kindness, and forsookest them not.'

'Only acknowledge thine iniquity, that thou hast transgressed against Jer. iii. 12, 13.
the Lord thy God ; . . . . for I am merciful, saith the Lord, and I will
not keep anger for ever.'

NOTE.—Parallel verses are too numerous for entry here.

Psalm LII

(*Nine Verses*)

\erses

In this Psalm the writer sharply reproaches the godless man, who
strengthened himself in his wickedness, because of the 'abundance of   7
his riches.' 'Why boastest thou thyself in mischief, O mighty man?'   1
He delights in evil more than in good, and falsehood rather than truth.
'O thou deceitful tongue !' The Psalmist comforts himself in his faith,   4
'like a green olive tree in the house of God.' 'I trust in the mercy of   8
God for ever and ever.' Thus he 'waits' on God.

PARALLEL VERSES

'I will cause the arrogancy of the proud to cease, and will lay low Isa. xiii. 11.
the haughtiness of the terrible.'

'They that see thee shall narrowly look upon thee, ... saying, Is Isa. xiv. 16.
this the man that made the earth to tremble, and did shake kingdoms?'

'The fear of the Lord is to hate evil : pride and arrogancy, and the Prov. viii. 13.
evil way, and the froward mouth, do I hate.'

Psalm LIII

(*Six Verses*)

\erse

This Psalm is almost word for word the same as the 14th Psalm
(see page 11), commencing 'The fool hath said in his heart, There is
no God.' 'Have the workers of iniquity no knowledge? who eat up my   1
people as they eat bread : they have not called upon God.' With

6 fervency the Psalmist exclaims, 'Oh, that the salvation of Israel were come out of Zion ! When God bringeth back the captivity of His people, Jacob shall rejoice, and Israel shall be glad.'

PARALLEL VERSES

Lam. iv. 22. 'The punishment of thine iniquity is accomplished, O daughter of Zion ; he will no more carry thee away into captivity. . . .'

Lam. v. 1, 2. 'Remember, O Lord, what is come upon us : . . . . our inheritance is turned to strangers. . . .'

Lam. v. 21. 'Turn Thou us unto Thee, O Lord, and we shall be turned.'

Isa. lxv. 19. 'I will rejoice in Jerusalem, and joy in My people.'

Psalm LIV

(*Seven Verses*)

Verses

The Psalmist gives expression to a perfect faith in God when

3 surrounded by 'oppressors,' who 'have not set God before them.'

4 'Hear my prayer, O God ; give ear to the words of my mouth.' 'God is mine helper ; . . . . He hath delivered me out of all trouble. . I will praise Thy name, O Lord ; for it is good.'

PARALLEL VERSES

2 Sam. xxii. 5. 'The floods of ungodly men made me afraid.   '

2 Sam. xxii. 7. 'In my distress I called upon the Lord, and cried to my God : and He did hear my voice out of His temple, and my cry did enter into His ears.'

Isa. xli. 10. 'Fear thou not ; for I am with thee : be not dismayed ; for I am thy God : I will strengthen thee : yea, I will help thee : yea, I will uphold thee with the right hand of My righteousness.'

Isa. xli. 13. 'Fear not, I will help thee.'

Psalm LV

(*Twenty-three Verses*)

Verses

This Psalm of David describes the anguish of one whose heart is

4 overwhelmed by injustice and persecution. His 'heart is sore pained' within him. The 'terrors of death are fallen' upon him. 'Horror

hath overwhelmed' him. He exclaimed, 'Oh, that I had wings like
a dove! for then would I fly away, and be at rest.' The Psalmist
felt deeply that it was not the enemy that reproached him, but it was
one who had been his friend and acquaintance, who had taken sweet
counsel with him, and 'walked unto the house of God in company.' In   14
a state of mental frenzy he appeals to God to avenge his cause.   15
After this he says, 'As for me, I will call upon God ; and the Lord shall   16
save me. Evening, morning, and at noon will I pray, and cry aloud :   17
and He shall hear my voice. He hath delivered my soul in peace from   18
the battle that was against me : for there were many with me.' The
Psalmist describes the deceit of the enemy, whose words were smoother   21
than butter, and softer than oil, whilst 'war was in his heart.' Again he
finds comfort in the words of his faith—'Cast thy burden upon the Lord,   22
and He shall sustain thee : He shall never suffer the righteous to be
moved.'

PARALLEL VERSES

'Now there was a long war between the house of Saul and the house   2 Sam. iii. 1.
of David ; but David waxed stronger and stronger, and the house of
Saul waxed weaker and weaker.'

'   The hypocrite's hope shall perish.'   Job viii. 13.

'   The triumphing of the wicked is short, and the joy of the   Job xx. 5.
hypocrite but for a moment.'

'An hypocrite with his mouth destroyeth his neighbour.'   Prov. xi. 9.

'   The counsels of the wicked are deceit.'   Prov. xII. 5.

'He that hateth dissembleth with his lips, and layeth up deceit with   Prov. xxvi. 24.
him : when he speaketh fair, believe him not.'

'. . . . They bend their tongues, like their bow, for lies ; but they   Jer. ix. 3.
are not valiant for the truth upon the earth : for they proceed from evil
to evil, and they know not Me, saith the Lord.'

Psalm LVI

(*Thirteen Verses*)

This Psalm, like the one which follows, is an appeal to God
for protection against the enemy. 'Be merciful unto me, O God :   1
for man would swallow me up ; he fighting daily oppresseth me.'

Verses

5   His faith rises. 'Every day they wrest my words; all their thoughts are against me for evil.' 'What time I am afraid, I will trust in Thee.' 'In God I will praise His word, in God I have put my trust ·

3   I will not fear what flesh can do unto me.' 'Put Thou my tears in Thy bottle.' Great is his faith. 'When I cry unto Thee, then shall mine enemies turn back ; *this I know* ; for God is for me.' He has

13   been spared from death. 'Wilt not Thou deliver my feet from falling, that I may walk before God in the light of the living ? '

PARALLEL VERSES

2 Kings xix. 15.   'And Hezekiah prayed before the Lord, and said, O Lord God of Israel, '

2 Kings xix. 16.   'Thou art the God, even Thou alone, Lord ; bow down Thine ear and hear ; open Thou, Lord, Thine eyes, and see ; and hear the words of Sennacherib.'

2 Kings xix. 19.   'Save Thou us out of his hand, that all the kingdoms of the earth may know that Thou art the Lord God, even Thou only.'

Prov. xv. 29.   'The Lord is far from the wicked ; but He heareth the prayer of the righteous.'

Jer. xxiii. 24.   'Can any hide himself in secret places that I shall not see him ? saith the Lord. Do not I fill heaven and earth ? saith the Lord.'

Psalm LVII

(*Eleven Verses*)
(See Psalm CVIII)

Verses

2   In circumstances of peculiar peril the Psalmist pours out his soul in prayer to God, saying, 'Yea, in the shadow of Thy wings will I make my refuge, until these calamities be overpast.' 'I will cry unto God most high, unto God that performeth all things for me.' After

7   describing his position, he exclaims : 'My heart is fixed, O God, my heart is fixed : I will sing and give praise. Awake, psaltery and harp.' Thus he sings praises to God.

PARALLEL VERSES ·

2 Sam. xxii. 47.   'The Lord liveth ; and blessed be my rock ; and exalted be the God of the rock of my salvation.'

'Thou hast delivered me from the violent man.' 2 Sam. xxii. 49.

'Therefore I will give thanks unto Thee, O Lord.   I will sing 2 Sam. xxii. 50.
praises unto Thy name.'

'Great is the Lord, and greatly to be praised.' 1 Chron. xvi.
25.

'Let the heavens be glad, let the earth rejoice.   And let men say 1 Chron. xvi.
31.
among the nations, The Lord reigneth.'

'Ezra the scribe stood upon a pulpit of wood·   . . . he opened the Neh. viii. 4, 5.
book in the sight of the people.'

'And Ezra blessed the Lord, the great God, and all the people Neh. viii. 6.
answered, Amen, Amen.'

'. . . . The joy of the Lord is your strength.' Neh. viii. 10.

'Sing unto the Lord a new song, and His praise to the end of the Isa. xlii. 10.
earth.'

Psalm LVIII

(*Eleven Verses*)

Verses

This Psalm is a protest against the wicked.   Their poison is like 3, 4
that of a serpent : they are deaf to instructing, and will not listen
to the 'voice of charmers, charming never so wisely.' Such is the 5
nature of the wicked.   The Psalmist prays for their destruction, that it
may be said, 'Verily He is a God that judgeth in the earth.'

PARALLEL VERSES

'. . . . Ascribe ye greatness unto our God. He is the rock, His work Deut. xxxii. 3,
4.
is perfect : for all His ways are judgment : a God of truth, and without
iniquity, just and right is He.'

'He is the Lord our God ; His judgments are in all the earth.' 1 Chron. xvi.
14.

'Doth God pervert judgment ? or doth the Almighty pervert justice ?' Job viii. 3.

'. . . . God shall bring every work unto judgment ; with every secret Ecc. xii. 14
thing, whether it be good, or whether it be evil.'

Psalm LIX

(*Seventeen Verses*)

Verses

The Psalmist prays for deliverance from his enemies. He de- 1
scribes their cruelty, ... the 'workers of iniquity'; how they 2

6, 14   go 'round about the city, and make a noise like a dog ·
swords are in their lips ; for who, say they, doth hear ? ' He prays,

11   'Scatter them, O Lord, by Thy power, O Lord our shield ;

13   and let them know that God ruleth in Jacob unto the ends of the earth.'

9, 16   'God is my defence.' 'I will sing of Thy power ; yea, I will sing aloud
of Thy mercy in the morning, ... my defence and refuge in the day

17   of my trouble. Unto Thee, O my strength, will I sing : for God is my
defence, and the God of my mercy.'

PARALLEL VERSES

Prov. v. 21, 22.   'The ways of man are before the eyes of the Lord, and He pon-
dereth all his goings. His own iniquities shall take the wicked himself, and he shall be holden with the cords of his sin.'

Mal. iii. 5.   '   I will come near to you to judgment.'

Mal. iii. 6.   '   For I am the Lord, I change not : therefore ye sons of
Jacob are not consumed.'

Psalm LX

(*Twelve Verses*)

Verses

This Psalm is full of historic allusions. The Psalmist is disheartened
after some great battle, yet he hopes in God that he will yet gain the

1   victory in the end. 'O God, Thou hast cast us off, Thou hast scattered

3   us, Thou hast been displeased ; O turn Thyself to us again. Thou

4   hast shewed Thy people hard things ; . . . . Thou hast given a banner
to them that fear Thee because of the truth.'

11, 12   'Give us help from trouble : for vain is the help of man. Through
God we shall do valiantly : for He it is that shall tread down our
enemies.'

PARALLEL VERSES

2 Sam. i. 11, 13.   After a great battle, when both Saul and his son Jonathan were
slain, David rent his clothes, 'mourned, and wept, and fasted until
even, for Saul, and for Jonathan his son, and for the people of the
Lord, and for the house of Israel ; because they were fallen by the
sword.'

'How are the mighty fallen in the midst of the battle, and the 2 Sam. i. 25, 27.
weapons of war perished!'

'And it came to pass after this, that David sought God in his great 2 Sam. ii. 1.
faith.'

Psalm LXI

(*Eight Verses*)

This is a prayer of personal consecration to God. 'I will abide
in Thy tabernacle for ever : I will trust in the covert of Thy wings.
For Thou, O God, hast heard my vows : Thou wilt prolong the king's   5, 6
life, and his years as many generations. He shall abide before God   7
for ever : O prepare mercy and truth, which may preserve him, ...
that I may daily perform my vows.' When his heart is overwhelmed   8
he will cry to God ·   'Lead me to the rock that is higher than I.'   2

PARALLEL VERSES

'David blessed the Lord before all the congregation : and David 1 Chron. xxix.
said, Blessed be Thou, Lord God of Israel our father, for ever and ever.'   10.

'The acts of David the king, first and last, are written in the book 1 Chron. xxix.
of Samuel the seer, book of Nathan the prophet, and in the book of   29.
Gad the seer.'

'The living, the living, he shall praise Thee, as I do this day : the Isa. xxxviii. 19
father to the children shall make known Thy truth.'

Psalm LXII

(*Twelve Verses*)

Here is expressed the perfect conception of the soul's union with
God, for He is the infinite One, in whom we 'live, move, and have
our being.' 'Truly my soul waiteth upon God : from Him cometh   1
my salvation. He is the rock of my strength, and my refuge is in God.
Trust in Him at all times, ye people, pour out your heart before   8
Him. . . . If riches increase, set not your heart upon them.' To God   10
belong both power and mercy : to every man He renders according to   12
his work.

Parallel Verses

Deut. iv. 39. 'The Lord He is God in heaven above, and upon the earth beneath; there is none else.'

Deut. x. 14. 'Behold the heaven and the heaven of heavens is the Lord's Thy God, the earth also, with all that therein is.'

1 Sam. ii. 2. 'There is none holy as the Lord; for there is none beside Thee · neither is there any rock like our God!'

1 Chron. xvi. 20. 'Give unto the Lord the glory due unto His name.'

Job ix. 19. 'If I speak of strength, lo, He is strong. He is not a man, as I am, that I should answer Him.'

Jer. x. 6. 'Forasmuch as there is none like unto Thee, O Lord; Thou art great in might.'

Dan. vi. 26. 'He is the living God.'

Habak. i. 12. 'Art Thou not from everlasting, O Lord my God, mine Holy One?

Habak. ii. 14. 'The earth shall be filled with the knowledge of the glory of the Lord, as the waters cover the sea.'

Habak. iii. 6. 'His ways are everlasting.'

Psalm LXIII

(*Eleven Verses*)

Verses

In this Psalm we perceive the intensity of the Psalmist's faith in God; it seems to bring us to the high-water mark of the spiritual genius of the Bible. The Psalmist exults in the conscious presence of God.

1 'My soul thirsteth for Thee; my flesh longeth for Thee in a dry and

8, 6 thirsty land, where no water is; my soul followeth hard after Thee.'

He remembers the time when on his bed in the night watches he medi-

3, 4 tated upon the lovingkindness of God 'which is better than life. . . .

7 Thus will I bless Thee while I live : because Thou hast been my help,

11 therefore in the shadow of Thy wings will I rejoice. . . .'

Parallel Verses

Isa. lv. 1. 'Ho, every one that thirsteth, come ye to the waters.'

Isa. lv. 3. 'Incline your ear, and come unto Me : hear, and your soul shall live; and I will make an everlasting covenant with you, even the sure mercies of David.'

Psalm LXIV

(*Ten Verses*)

In this appeal to God for protection against the enemy, the Psalmist describes the condition of the godless man. 'Hide me from the secret counsel of the wicked,' the 'workers of iniquity.' They 'whet their tongue like a sword. They bend their bows to shoot in secret at the perfect   and fear not.' They talk of 'laying snares privily,' saying, ' Who shall see them ?' They ignore the presence of God. 'They search out iniquities ; they accomplish a diligent search : but God shall shoot at them. . . . Suddenly shall they be wounded. So shall they make their own tongue '—'even bitter words '—'fall upon themselves.' 'The righteous shall be glad in the Lord, and shall trust in Him ; and all the upright in heart shall glory.'

2

3, 4

5

6

7

8, 3

10

PARALLEL VERSES

The triumphing of the wicked is short, and the joy of the hypocrite but for a moment.' — Job xx. 5.

'Is not God in the height of heaven ? and behold the height of the stars, how high they are l and thou sayest, How doth God know ?' — Job xxii. 12, 13.

'What is the hope of the hypocrite, though he hath gained, when God taketh away his soul ?' — Job xxvii. 8.

'The righteousness of the perfect shall direct his way : but the wicked shall fall by his own wickedness.' — Prov. xi. 5.

'. . . . The counsels of the wicked are deceit. . . . The wicked is snared by the transgression of his lips.' — Prov. xii. 5, 13.

' They are not valiant for the truth upon the earth : they proceed from evil to evil, and they know not Me, saith the Lord.' — Jer. ix. 3.

Psalm LXV

(*Thirteen Verses*)

This is a beautiful hymn of praise to God, poetical and musical. 'O Thou that hearest prayer, unto Thee shall all flesh come. . . . Blessed is

1

4

Verses

5   the man ' who dwells ' in Thy courts, ... O God of our salvation, who art the confidence of all the ends of the earth, and of them that

8   are afar off upon the sea. . . . Thou makest the morning and evening

11   rejoice. . . . Thou crownest the year with Thy goodness : . . . . Thy

12   paths drop fatness . . . . upon the pastures of the wilderness : . . . . the

13   little hills rejoice on every side. The pastures are clothed with flocks ; the valleys also are covered with corn ; they shout for joy, they also sing.'

PARALLEL VERSES

Prov. x. 28.   ' The hope of the righteous shall be gladness.'

Isa. xxv. 1.   ' O Lord, Thou art my God ; I will praise Thy name, for Thou hast done wonderful things.'

Isa. xxv. 4.   ' For Thou hast been a strength to the poor, a strength to the needy in his distress, a refuge from the storm, a shadow from the heat, when the blast of the terrible ones is as a storm against the wall.'

Isa. lxi. 10.   '   I will greatly rejoice : my soul shall be joyful in my God.'

Psalm LXVI

(*Twenty Verses*)

Verses

This is a soul-inspiring hymn of praise addressed to ' all lands.'

' All the earth shall worship Thee, and shall sing unto Thee ; they shall sing to Thy name.' The Psalmist now records God's wonders of

6   old ' towards the children of men,' when He ' turned the sea into dry land : they walked through the flood on foot : then did we rejoice in

7, 9   Him. He ruleth by His power for ever ' ; He ' holdeth our soul in

10, 11, 12   life.' We are proved and tried, as ' silver is tried,' by means of affliction.

16–20   The Psalmist appeals to all who fear God, saying, ' I will declare what He hath done for my soul. I cried to Him with my mouth, and extolled Him with my tongue. If I regard iniquity in my heart, the Lord will not hear me : but verily God hath heard me ; He hath attended to the voice of my prayer. Blessed be God, which hath not turned away my prayer, nor His mercy from me.'

'And the children of Israel went into the midst of the sea upon the Ex. xiv. 22. dry ground : and the waters were a wall unto them, on their right hand, and on their left.'

'Then sang Moses and the children of Israel this song unto the Ex. xvi. 1, 2. Lord :   . . The Lord is my strength and song, and is become my salvation : He is my God, ... my fathers' God, and I will exalt Him.'

'Who is like unto Thee, O Lord, among the gods ? Who is like Ex. xvi. 11. unto Thee, glorious in holiness, fearful in praises, doing wonders ? '

'Thou in Thy mercy hast led forth the people which Thou hast Ex. xvi. 13. redeemed. Thou hast guided them in Thy strength unto Thy holy habitation.'

Psalm LXVII

(Seven Verses)   Verses

This is a joyous appeal to all the nations of the earth to join in prayer and praise to God : 'Let the people praise Thee, O God ; let   3 all the people praise Thee. Let the nations be glad and sing for joy.'   4 The Psalmist prays that the face of God may 'shine upon us ' ; that His   1, 2 ways 'may be known upon earth. . . . Then shall the earth yield her   6 increase, and God, even our own God, shall bless us. God shall bless   7 us ; and all the ends of the earth shall fear Him.'

'Hannah said, ... I have poured out my soul before the Lord ; 1 Sam. i. 15. 18. . . and her countenance was no more sad.'

'My heart rejoiceth in the Lord. I rejoice in Thy salvation. 1 Sam. ii. 1, 2. There is none holy as the Lord ; for there is none beside Thee · neither is there any rock like our God.'

'I will greatly rejoice in the Lord ; my soul shall be joyful in my Isa. lxi. 10. God.'

'The Lord God will cause righteousness and praise to spring forth Isa. lxi. 11. before all the nations.'

'And all nations shall call you blessed : for ye shall be a delight- Mal. iii. 12. some land, saith the Lord of Hosts.'

Psalm LXVIII

(Thirty-five Verses)

Verses

This Psalm is an outburst of enthusiasm in the worship of God and indignation against God's enemies. 'As smoke is driven away, so drive them away. . . . But let the righteous be glad, let them rejoice before God : yea, let them exceedingly rejoice. Sing unto God, sing praises to His name. . . . A father of the fatherless, and a judge of the widows, is God in His holy habitation.' The Psalmist takes a mental glance back at Israel's history, when God led His people through the wilderness : . . . . even Sinai itself was moved at the presence of God, the God of Israel.' 'Thou, O God, hast prepared of Thy goodness for the poor.' In language of poetic beauty the Psalmist says, 'Though ye have lien among the pots, yet shall ye be as the wings of a dove covered with silver, and her feathers with yellow gold. . . . The chariots of God are twenty thousand, even thousands of angels, ... as in Sinai.' God is among them, in 'the holy place.' 'Blessed be the Lord, who daily loadeth us with benefits, even the God of our salvation   He that is our God is the God of salvation ; and unto God the Lord belong the issues from death.' He mentions a musical procession 'in the Temple'; 'the singers' went first, the 'players on instruments followed after ; among them were the damsels playing with timbrels. Bless ye God in the congregations.' . 'Scatter Thou the people that delight in war.' 'Sing unto God, ye kingdoms of the earth : O sing praises unto the Lord.'

Verse numbers in left margin: 3, 4, 5, 7, 8, 10, 17, 19, 20, 24, 25, 26, 30, 32

PARALLEL VERSES

'When the children of Israel were gone forth out of the land of Egypt, the same day came they unto the wilderness of Sinai. . . . The Lord called unto him (Moses) saying : Thus shalt thou say to the house of Jacob, and tell the children of Israel ; ye have seen . . : . how I bare you on eagle's wings and brought you unto Myself ;   ye shall be unto Me a kingdom of priests, a holy nation.'

'The Lord your God, which goeth before you, He shall fight for you. . . . Thou hast seen how that the Lord thy God bare thee, as a man doth bear his son.'

Reference numbers in left margin: Ex. xix. 1. / Ex. xix. 3. / Ex. xix. 4. / Ex. xix. 6. / Deut. i. 30, 31.

'He kept him as the apple of His eye.   As an eagle stirreth up   Deut. xxxii. 10, her nest, fluttereth over her young, spreadeth abroad her wings : . . . .   11. so the Lord alone did lead him (Israel). . . .'

'This people have I formed for myself ; they shall shew forth my   Isa. xliii. 21. praise.'

Psalm LXIX

(*Thirty-six Verses*)

                                                                              Verses

Here the Psalmist gives expression to some overwhelming troubles.   1, 2 'Save me, O God : for the waters have come in unto my soul. I sink in deep mire, where there is no standing : I am come into deep waters,   3 where the floods overflow me. I am weary of my crying : my throat is   4 dried : mine eyes fail while I wait for my God.' He enters into the details of his miseries, and confesses his 'foolishness' and his 'sins.'   6 He prays that for his sake none who seek God may be 'ashamed' or 'confounded.' He is keenly sensitive to 'shame' and 'reproach'; and   7-12 complains that his acts of religious 'zeal' were made a subject of reproach against him. Thus he became a 'proverb,' and the 'song of the drunkards.'

      Now again he pours out his soul to God in prayer : 'Hear me,   13-19 O Lord : for Thy lovingkindness is good. Turn unto me according to the multitude of Thy tender mercies.' He finds comfort in the knowledge that these 'reproaches,' which have 'broken' his 'heart' and filled it with 'heaviness,' are all known to God. In vain he looked for some to 'take pity' and for 'comforters,' but he found   20 none. With these thoughts he loses his balance of mind, and he gives full vent to human wrath. Finally he recovers his faith in God,   29-36 believing that the 'Lord heareth the poor, and despiseth not His   33 prisoners.' He believes in the future of Zion ; for 'God will save Zion, and will build the cities of Judah : that they may dwell there, and have it   35 in possession.' The 'seed also of His servants' shall 'inherit' it, and   36 they that love His name shall dwell therein.

2 Sam. xxii. 17.   'He sent from above, He took me; He drew me out of many waters.'

2 Sam. xxii. 18.   He delivered me from my strong enemy, and from them that hated me.'

2 Sam. xxii. 19.   'They prevented me in the day of my calamity : but the Lord was my stay.'

Job v. 7.   'Man is born unto trouble, as the sparks fly upward.'

Job v. 19.   ' 'He shall deliver thee in six troubles ; yea, in seven there shall no evil touch thee.'

Job vi. 14.   'To him that is afflicted pity should be showed from his friend.'

Jer. xvi. 7.   'Mine eyes are upon all their ways ; they are not hid from my

Jer. xvi. 17.   face. . . . Neither is their iniquity hid from mine eyes. . . . O Lord,

Jer. xvi. 19.   my strength, and my fortress, and my refuge in the day of affliction.'

Psalm LXX

(Five Verses)

Verse

In these few verses the Psalmist appeals to God to make a speedy end to the persecutions to which he is subject, and to avenge his cause. He prays that all those who seek God may 'rejoice and be glad,' and such as 'love Thy salvation say continually, Let God be magnified.'

5   'I am poor and needy : make haste unto me, O God ; Thou art my help and my deliverer ; O Lord, make no tarrying.

Job xi. 16.   'Thou shalt forget thy misery, and remember it as waters that pass away.'

Lam. iii. 31, 33.   'The Lord will not cast off for ever.   He doth not afflict willingly, nor grieve the children of men.'

Nahum i. 7.   'The Lord is good, a stronghold in the day of trouble; and He knoweth them that trust in Him.'

Psalm LXXI

(*Twenty-four Verses*)

This Psalm is one of prayer and meditation, the utterances of a matured life of many experiences. The Psalmist says, 'Thou art my hope, O Lord God ; Thou art my trust from my youth.' From birth he has been upheld by God. 'My praise shall be continually of Thee.' 'I am as a wonder unto many ; but Thou art my strong refuge.' The Psalmist contemplates the time of old age, when his strength will fail him. But he will hope continually, and will yet praise God more and more. 'O God, Thou hast taught me from my youth : and hitherto have I declared Thy wondrous works. Now also when I am old and grey-headed, O God, forsake me not, until I have shewed Thy strength unto this generation, and Thy power to every one that is to come. . . . O God, who is like unto Thee?

Although he has seen 'great and sore troubles,' yet his faith has never failed him ; so now with joyous song he declares, 'I will also praise Thee with the psaltery ·   unto Thee will I sing with the harp, O Thou Holy One of Israel. My lips greatly rejoice when I sing unto Thee ; and my soul, which Thou hast redeemed. My tongue also shall talk of Thy righteousness all the day long.'

	5
	6
	7
	9
	14
	17
	'
	19, 20
	22, 23
	24

PARALLEL VERSES

'For who is God, save the Lord ? and who is a rock, save our God ? God is my strength and power : and He maketh my way perfect.'   2 Sam. xxii. 32, 33.

'   And he (Solomon) said : Lord God of Israel, there is no God like Thee, in heaven above, or on earth beneath.'   1 Kings viii. 23.

'Sing unto the Lord, all the earth : shew forth from day to day His salvation. . . . For great is the Lord, and greatly to be praised. Give unto the Lord the glory due unto His name.'   1 Chron. xvi. 23. 1 Chron. xvi. 25, 29.

'Let the Lord be glorified.'   Isa. xvi. 5.

'His glory covered the heavens, and the earth was full of His praise.'   Habak. iii. 3.

Psalm LXXII

(Twenty Verses. 'A Psalm for Solomon')

This composition, headed 'A Psalm for Solomon,' appears to be a prophetic prayer written by his father, King David. Great gifts of a spiritual kind are predicted, not only for his son but for the future of the kingdom of Israel, indicating the universal destiny of the religion of Israel. 'Give the king Thy judgments, O God, and Thy righteousness unto the king's son. He shall judge Thy people with righteousness, and Thy poor with judgment.' The Psalmist foresees a reign of peace and prosperity, through the wisdom and judgment of his son Solomon : 'He shall have dominion also from sea to sea, and from the river unto the ends of the earth. . . . All kings shall fall down before him : and all nations shall serve him. . . . Prayer shall be made for him continually ; and daily shall he be praised.' His reign shall be so prosperous that an handful of corn 'upon the top of mountains, the fruit thereof shall shake like Lebanon ·   . and they of the city shall flourish like grass of the earth. His name shall endure for ever : all nations shall call him blessed. Blessed be the Lord God, the God of Israel ; . . . . and let the whole earth be filled with His glory ; Amen and Amen. The prayers of David the son of Jesse are ended.'

1

8

11

15

16

17

18

19

20

Parallel Verses

2 Sam. xxiii. 1.   'Now these be the last words of David. David the son of Jesse said, and the man who was raised up on high, the anointed of the God of Jacob, and the sweet psalmist of Israel said,'

2 Sam. xxiii. 2.   'The Spirit of the Lord spake by me, and His word was in my tongue.'

2 Sam. xxiii. 3.   'The God of Israel said, the rock of Israel spake to me, He that ruleth over men must be just, ruling in the fear of God.'

1 Kings ii. 1.   'Now the days of David drew nigh that he should die : and he charged Solomon his son, saying,'

1 Kings ii. 3.   'I go the way of all the earth : be thou strong, therefore, and show thyself a man : and keep the charge of the Lord thy God, to walk in His ways, to keep His statutes, and His commandments, ... as it is written in the law of Moses.'

'And all the earth sought to Solomon, to hear his wisdom, which 1 Kings x. 24.
God had put in his heart.'

' Then Solomon sat on the throne of the Lord as king instead of 1 Chron. xxix.
David his father, and prospered : and all Israel obeyed him.' 23.

'And the Lord magnified Solomon exceedingly in the sight of all 1 Chron. xxix.
Israel.' 25.

' Thus David the son of Jesse reigned over all Israel.' 1 Chron. xxix.
26.
' And he died in a good old age, full of days, riches, and honour ; 1 Chron. xxix.
and Solomon his son reigned in his stead.' 28.

Psalm LXXIII

(*Twenty-eight Verses.* '*A Psalm of Asaph*') Verses

This Psalm has been written by one who is deeply impressed by
the inequalities of life ; he contemplates the prosperity of the wicked,
their apparent strength and freedom from the troubles of the world,
their 'pride,' and overbearing treatment of the helpless ; and they
say, 'How doth God know ?' Thus it is that they oppress and per- 11
secute their fellow men. Whilst the Psalmist utters this soliloquy
he feels within himself the temptation almost to 'envy' such pro- 3
sperity, considering the sufferings of the righteous man until the 5
thought becomes 'too painful' for him. Then he enters the sanctuary of God, and his eyes become open to the true position ; 17
it was not until he did so that he perceived that the life of the godless
man is but for the time being ; because he has ignored the 'image
of God' in his soul. Now he reproaches himself for his mistaken
views, and exclaims : 'Thou shalt guide me with Thy counsel, 24
and afterwards receive me to glory. Whom have I in heaven but 25
Thee ? and there is none upon earth that I desire beside Thee.'
Though his 'flesh' and his 'heart' may fail him, yet God will remain 6
his 'strength,' and his 'portion for ever' ; therefore it is good for him
to 'draw near to God.' 'I have put my trust in the Lord God, that I 28
may declare all Thy works.'

PARALLEL VERSES

' Will ye speak wickedly for God? and talk deceitfully for him ?' Job xiii 7

Job xx. 5.   'The triumphing of the wicked is short, and the joy of the hypocrite but for a moment.'

Jer. ix. 23, 24.   'Thus saith the Lord, Let not the wise man glory in his wisdom, neither let the mighty man glory in his might, let not the rich man glory in his riches : but let him that glorieth glory in this, that he understandeth and knoweth Me, that I am the Lord which exercise lovingkindness, judgment, and righteousness in the earth : for in these things I delight, saith the Lord.'

Gen. i. 27.   'God created man in His own image, in the image of God created He him.'

Psalm LXXIV

(*Twenty-three Verses*)

Verses

3

7

8

10

    The Psalmist expresses a bitter lamentation because of the desolations that surround him : 'They have cast fire into Thy sanctuary ; they have burned up all the synagogues of God in the land. . . . O God, how long shall the adversary reproach ? shall the enemy blaspheme Thy name for ever ? '

12

16

17

    After this lament, his faith revives : 'For God is my King of old, working salvation in the midst of the earth. . . . The day is Thine, the night also is Thine : Thou hast prepared the light and the sun. . . . Thou hast made summer and winter.'

21–23

    The Psalmist concludes in prayer : ' O let not the oppressed return ashamed : let the poor and needy praise Thy name.'

PARALLEL VERSES

Lam. ii. 1.   ' How hath the Lord covered the daughter of Zion with a cloud in His anger, and cast down from heaven unto earth the beauty of Israel.'

Lam. iii. 22.   ' It is of the Lord's mercies that we are not consumed, because His compassions fail not.'

Lam. iii. 23.   'They are new every morning : great is Thy faithfulness.'

Lam. iii. 24.   'The Lord is my portion, saith my soul ; therefore will I hope in Him.'

Lam. iii. 25.
Lam. iii. 31.   'The Lord is good unto them that wait for Him, to the soul that seeketh Him ; . . . . for the Lord will not cast off for ever.'

Psalm LXXV

(*Ten Verses. '' A Psalm or Song of Asaph'*)

This is a joyous hymn of praise and faith in God. 'Unto Thee, O God, do we give thanks. . . I said unto the fools, Deal not foolishly ; and to the wicked, Lift not up the horn : . . . . speak not with a stiff neck. For promotion cometh neither from the east, nor from the west, nor from the south. But God is the judge : He putteth down one, and setteth up another. . . . I will sing praises to the God of Jacob.'

1
4
5
6
7

PARALLEL VERSES

'And he (David) appointed certain of the Levites to minister before the ark of the Lord, and to record, and to thank and praise the Lord God of Israel : Asaph the chief ; next to him Zechariah,' &c., 'with psalteries and with harps ; but Asaph made a sound with cymbals.' — 1 Chron. xvi. 4.

' 1 Chron. xvi. 5.

'   . On that day David delivered first this psalm to thank the Lord into the hand of Asaph and his brethen.' — 1 Chron. xvi. 7.

'Give thanks unto the Lord, call upon His name, make known His deeds among the people.' — 1 Chron. xvi. 8.

'Sing unto Him, sing psalms unto Him, talk ye of all His wondrous works,' &c. — 1 Chron. xvi. 9.

Psalm LXXVI

(*Twelve Verses*)

Verses

A tribute of praise and reverence to the Almighty, who governs 'princes' and the 'kings of the earth.' 'In Judah is God known ; His name is great in Israel, His dwelling place in Zion.' This psalm testifies to the universality of the religion of Zion.

1, 2

PARALLEL VERSES

'   Know that there is none like me in all the earth.' — Ex. ix. 14.

'Thy right hand, O Lord, is become glorious in power: . and in the greatness of Thine excellency, thou hast overthrown them that rose up against Thee.' — Ex. xv. 6. / Ex. xv. 7.

1 Kings viii.
60.

‘   That all the people of the earth may know that the Lord is
God, and there is none else.’

Isa. xii. 5, 6.   ‘ Sing unto the Lord ; for He hath done excellent things : this is
known in all the earth.   Cry out and shout, thou inhabitant of Zion
for great is the Holy One of Israel in the midst of thee.’

Psalm LXXVII

(*Twenty Verses*)

Verses

2   The Psalmist pours out his heart in the ‘ day of his trouble.’ He
3   could find no comfort, his spirit was so overwhelmed that he could
4   not sleep, day or night.   During a wakeful night he meditates on the
5   ‘ years of ancient times,’ he communes with his own heart—‘ my spirit
6   made diligent search ’—and he asks himself a series of questions :
7   Will the Lord cast off for ever ? Will He be favourable no more ?
8   Is His mercy clean gone for ever ? Doth His promise fail for ever-
9   more ? Hath God forgotten to be gracious ? Hath He in anger shut
up His tender mercies ?

He comes to the conclusion that to question for a moment the
infinite power, lovingkindness, and mercy of God is due to a lack of
10   faith in himself, and says, ‘ This is my infirmity.’   After this he
12   meditates on the works of God. ‘ Thy way, O God, is in the
13   sanctuary : who is so great a God as our God ? ’ ‘ Thy way is in
19   the sea, and Thy path in the great waters, and Thy footsteps are
20   not known.   Thou leddest Thy people like a flock by the hand of
Moses and Aaron.’

Parallel Verses

Jos. i. 8.   ‘ This book of the law shall not depart out of thy mouth ; but thou
shalt meditate therein day and night.’

Job v. 8.   ‘ I would seek unto God, and unto God would I commit my cause.

Jer. x. 12.   ‘ He hath made the earth by His power, He hath established the
world by His wisdom, and hath stretched out the heavens by His discretion.’

Eccles. vii. 14.   ‘ In the day of prosperity be joyful, but in the day of adversity consider.’

God will not cast away a perfect man.'   Job viii.2.

'He is not a man, as I am, that I should answer Him, and we should   Job iv. 32.
come together in judgment.'

Psalm LXXVIII

(Seventy-two Verses)

Verses

This Psalm is a summary of the history of the children of Israel.
Give ear, O my people, ... I will utter dark sayings of old, 'which   1, 2
we have heard and known, and our fathers have told us.'   The Psalmist   3
desires to transmit his knowledge to generations to come, so that   4, 5
children which shall be born shall arise and teach their children, that   6
they may learn to hope in God, and not forget the works of God, but   7
keep His commandments, that they may 'not be as their fathers, a   8
stubborn and rebellious generation, a generation that set not their heart
aright, and whose spirit was not steadfast with God.'   'Marvellous   12
things did He in the sight of their fathers, in the land of Egypt ·
He divided the sea, and caused them to pass through ; and He made   13, 14
the waters to stand as an heap. . . . He led them with a cloud by day,
and all the night with a light of fire.'   Yet they said, 'Can God furnish   19
a table in the wilderness?'   This want of faith was equivalent to speaking
'against God,' 'because they believed not in God, and trusted not in   22
His salvation ' : though He had commanded the clouds from above, and   23
opened the doors of heaven, and had rained down manna upon them to   24
eat, and had given them of the corn of heaven.   Man did eat angels'   25
food : He sent them meat to the full.   When great trouble came upon   34
them, then they returned and sought God.   And they remembered that   35
God was their rock, and the high God their Redeemer, but 'their heart   37
was not right with Him, neither were they steadfast in His covenant.   38
But He, being full of compassion, forgave their iniquity, and destroyed
them not. .   For He remembered that they were but flesh ; a wind   39
that passeth away, and cometh not again.'   After a graphic description   60-67
of the horrors that came upon the people, the Psalmist says : ' He   68
(God) chose the tribe of Judah, the Mount Zion, which He loved.
He chose David also His servant, and took him from the sheepfolds: 70

Verse
72

from following the ewes. . . . He brought him to feed Jacob His people, and Israel His inheritance, ... according to the integrity of his heart, and the skilfulness of his hands.'

PARALLEL VERSES

x. xix. 1.

'In the third month, when the children of Israel were gone forth out of the land of Egypt, the same day came they into the wilderness of Sinai.'

x. xix. 3.

'Thus shalt thou say of the name of Jacob, and tell the children of Israel : '

x. xix. 5.

'If ye will obey My voice indeed, and keep My covenant, then ye shall be a peculiar treasure unto Me above all people : for all the earth is Mine · '

x. xix. 6.

'And ye shall be unto Me a kingdom of priests, and a holy nation. These are the words which thou shalt speak unto the children of Israel.'

Sam. xvi. 1.

'And the Lord said unto Samuel,   Fill thine horn with oil, and go, I will send thee to Jesse ; . . . . for I have provided Me a king among his sons.'

Sam. xvi. 13.

'. . . . Then Samuel took the horn of oil, and appointed him in the midst of his brethren.'

Sam. vii. 8.

'   Say unto My servant David, Thus saith the Lord of Hosts, I took thee from the sheepcote, from following the sheep, to be ruler over My people, over Israel.'

Sam. vii. 26.

'Let Thy name be magnified for ever, saying, The Lord of hosts is the God over Israel : and let the house of My servant David be established before Thee.'

Psalm LXXIX

(*Thirteen Verses*)

Verses

1

10

This Psalm bears evidence of a much later date than many others. The Psalmist describes the desolation of Jerusalem, and 'Thy holy temple they have defiled.' He feels acutely the 'reproach' to which his nation is exposed, when the heathen ask 'Where is their God?' He prays that in the greatness of God's power, the 'sighing of the prisoner' may ascend to Him, and that those

Verse

who are already condemned to death may be spared! Finally
the Psalmist uses these words : 'So we Thy people and sheep of   13
Thy pasture will give Thee thanks for ever; we will shew forth
Thy praise to all generations.'

PARALLEL VERSES

'How doth the city sit solitary, that was full of people! How is   Lam. i. 1.
she become as a widow! she that was great among the nations,
and princess among the provinces, how is she become tributary!'

'O Lord, behold my affliction; for the enemy hath magnified   Lam. i. 9.
himself.'

'For these things I weep.'   Lam. i. 16.

'Zion spreadeth forth her hands, and there is none to comfort her.' Lam. i. 17.

'Behold, O Lord ; for I am in distress.'   Lam. i. 20.

'What thing shall I liken to thee, O daughter of Jerusalem?'   Lam. ii. 13.

'I called upon Thy name, O Lord, out of the low dungeon. Thou   Lam. iii. 55,
hast heard my voice; hide not Thine ear at my breathing, at my cry.'   56.

'Remember, O Lord, what is come upon us ; consider, and behold   Lam. v. 1.
our reproach.'

'Our inheritance is turned to strangers.'   Lam. v. 2.

'Thou, O Lord, remainest for ever ; Thy throne from generation   Lam. v. 19.
to generation.'

'Turn Thou us unto Thee, O Lord, and we shall be turned : renew   Lam. v. 21.
our days as of old.'

Psalm LXXX

(*Nineteen Verses*)

Verses

This Psalm deals with the same subject as the previous one—it
refers to the early history of Israel, when God planted the children of
Jacob in a heathen land, 'a vine out of Egypt'; now all is destruction,   8
God's vineyard cut down, burned with fire: 'they perished at the   16
rebuke of Thy countenance.' 'Return, we beseech Thee, O God of   14
hosts : look down from heaven, and behold, and visit this vine.'
Three times over the Psalmist exclaims : 'Turn us again, O God of   3, 7, 19
hosts, and cause Thy face to shine ; and we shall be saved. Quicken   18
us, and we will call upon Thy name.'

Isa. xxvii. 2.   'In that day sing ye unto her, a vineyard of red wine.'

Isa. xxvii. 3.   'I the Lord do keep it ; I will water it every moment : lest any hurt it, I will keep it night and day.'

Isa. xxvii. 6.   'He shall cause them that come of Jacob to take root : Israel shall blossom and bud, and fill the face of the world with fruit.'

Jer. xii. 2.   'Thou hast planted them, yea, they have taken root : they grow, yea, they bring forth fruit.'

Jer. xii. 10.   'Many pastors have destroyed my vineyard. They have made

Jer. xii. 11.   it desolate, and being desolate it mourneth unto Me ; the whole land is made desolate.'

Psalm LXXXI

(*Sixteen Verses*)

Verses

-     A joyous hymn of praise. 'Sing aloud unto God our strength :

2   make a joyous noise unto the God of Jacob. Take a psalm,' with 'timbrel,' 'harp,' 'psaltery,' and 'trumpet.' It solemnly pro-

8   tests against idolatrous tendencies : 'There shall no strange god be in thee ; neither shalt thou worship any strange god. I am the Lord thy God, which brought thee out of the land of Egypt ·

11   open thy mouth wide.   . But My people would not hearken to

13   My voice. Oh that My people had hearkened unto Me, and Israel had walked in My ways !' To neglect of God's holy laws the Psalmist attributes all their afflictions.

Ex. xx. 1.   'And God spake all these words saying, I am the Lord thy God, which have brought thee out of the land of Egypt, out of the house of bondage. Thou shalt have no other God before Me.'

Isa. xli. 16.   '. . . . Thou shalt rejoice in the Lord, and shalt glory in the Holy One of Israel.'

Isa. lxi. 10.   'I will greatly rejoice in the Lord, my soul shall be joyful in my God. . . .'

Isa. lxv. 14.   'Behold, my servants shall sing for joy of heart.'

' Thus saith the Lord : Sing with gladness for Jacob, and Jer. xxxi. 7.
shout among the chief of the nations : publish ye, praise ye, and say,
O Lord, save Thy people, the remnant of Israel.'

'Sing, O daughter of Zion : shout, O Israel : be glad and rejoice Zeph. iii. 14.
with all the heart, O daughter of Jerusalem.'

'Sing and rejoice, O daughter of Zion.' Zech. ii. 10.

Psalm LXXXII
(*Eight Verses*)

Verses

This is a Psalm that proclaims justice and judgment. ' How 2
long will ye judge unjustly, and accept the persons of the wicked?
Defend the poor and fatherless : do justice to the afflicted and 3
needy. Deliver the poor and needy : rid them out of the hand of the 4
wicked. . . . They walk on in darkness : all the foundations of the earth 5
are out of course. . . . But ye shall die like men. . . . ' Arise, O God, 7
judge the earth : for Thou shalt inherit all nations.'

PARALLEL VERSES

'Shall not the judge of all the earth do right?' Gen. xviii. 25.

' The Lord your God is God of gods, and Lord of lords, a Deut. x. 17.
great God, a mighty, and a terrible, which regardeth not persons, nor
taketh reward.'

' He doth execute the judgment of the fatherless and widow, and Deut. x. 18.
loveth the stranger, in giving him food and raiment.'

' Love ye therefore the stranger : for ye were strangers in the land Deut. x. 19.
of Egypt.'

' It is joy to the just to do judgment : but destruction shall be to Prov. xxi. 15.
the workers of iniquity.'

' I am the Lord, which exercise lovingkindness, judgment, Jer. ix. 24
and righteousness in the earth : for in these things I delight, saith the
Lord.'

Psalm LXXXIII
(*Eighteen Verses*)

Verses

Here is expressed an indignant protest against the persecutors of Israel. ' They have said, Come, and let us cut them off 4

Verses

12

13

18

from being a nation ; that the name of Israel may be no more in remembrance.   Let us take to ourselves the houses of God in possession.' The Psalmist prays 'that men may know that Thou, whose name alone is Jehovah, art the most high over all the earth.'

Parallel Verses

Isa. xii. 2.   'Behold, God is my salvation ; I will trust, and not be afraid : for the Lord Jehovah is my strength and my song ; He also is become my salvation.'

Isa. xii. 4.   'In that day shall ye say, Praise the Lord, call upon His name,' &c.

Isa. xiv. 27, 26.   'For the Lord of hosts hath purposed, and who shall disannul it ? and His hand is stretched out, and who shall turn it back ?'

Psalm LXXXIV

(*Twelve Verses*)

Verses

10

11

12

The Psalmist pours out his heart and soul in longing after God. He would rather be a 'doorkeeper' in the house of his God than 'dwell in the tents of wickedness.' 'For the Lord God is a sun and shield : the Lord will give grace and glory : no good thing will He withhold from them that walk uprightly.' He exclaims : 'O Lord of hosts, blessed is the man that trusteth in Thee.'

Parallel Verses

Deut. iv. 29.   '   Thou shalt seek the Lord thy God. . .   If thou seek Him

Deut. iv. 31.   with all thy heart and with all thy soul (For the Lord thy God is a merciful God ;) He will not forsake thee.'

Prov. xxviii. 5.   '. . . . They that seek the Lord understand all things.'

Hos. xii. 6.   '   Turn thou to thy God : keep mercy and judgment, and wait on thy God continually.'

Hos. xiv. 5, 6, 7.   'I will be as the dew unto Israel : his branches shall spread. They shall revive as corn, and grow as the vine.'

Hos. xiv. 9.   'Who is wise, and he shall understand these things ? . . . . the ways of the Lord are right ; and the just shall walk in them.'

Psalm LXXXV

(*Thirteen Verses*)   Verses

The Psalmist meditates during a respite from national trouble.   6
He prays fervently for a spiritual revival : . . . . 'that Thy people may
rejoice in Thee.' He listens to the voice of God, for he knows that God
will 'speak peace to His people, and to His saints,' but they must 'not   8
turn again to folly. . . . Mercy, truth, righteousness, and peace have   10
kissed each other. Truth shall spring out of the earth; and   11
righteousness shall look down from heaven. Yea, the Lord will give   12
us that which is good. Our land shall yield her increase,' whilst   13
'righteousness . . shall set us in the way of His steps.'

PARALLEL VERSES

'Behold, I have taught you statutes and judgments, even as the   Deut. iv. 5.
Lord my God commanded me, that ye should do so in the land whither
ye go to possess it.'

'Keep therefore and do them, for this is your wisdom and under-   Deut. iv. 6.
standing in the sight of the nations, which shall hear all these statutes,
and say, Surely this great nation is a wise and understanding people.'

'The Lord your God is gracious and merciful, and will not turn   2 Chron. xxx.
away His face from you, if ye return unto Him.'   9.

'He that followeth after righteousness and mercy findeth life,   Prov. xxi. 21
righteousness, and honour.'

'Open ye the gates, that the righteous nation, which keepeth the   Isa. xxvi. 2, 3.
truth, may enter in. Thou wilt keep him in perfect peace, whose mind
is stayed on Thee : because he trusteth in Thee.'

Psalm LXXXVI

(*Seventeen Verses*)   Verses

This Psalm, headed ' A prayer of David,' is an outpouring of the soul
expressed in the same words as in the thirty-first Psalm (verse 2) : ' Bow   1
down Thine ear, O Lord, hear me.' The distress is great—the Psalmist
says : 'I am poor and needy,' but his faith is great : ' for Thou, Lord,   5

F

Verses

6, 7   art good, and ready to forgive; and plenteous in mercy unto all them that call upon Thee. Give ear, O Lord, unto my prayer. . . . In the day of my trouble I will call upon Thee : for Thou wilt answer me.

10   . . . Thou art great, and doest wondrous things : Thou art God alone.

11, 12   Teach me Thy way, O Lord ; I will walk in Thy truth. . . . I will praise

13   Thee, O Lord my God, with all my heart.   . For great is Thy mercy

15   towards me. . . Thou, O Lord, art a God full of compassion, and

16   gracious, longsuffering, and plenteous in mercy and truth. . . . give

17   Thy strength unto Thy servant.' The Psalmist asks for a 'token for good ; . . . . because Thou hast holpen me, and comforted me.'

PARALLEL VERSES

1 Chron. xxviii. 9.   '. . . . The Lord searcheth all hearts, and understandeth all the imaginations of the thoughts : if thou seek Him, He will be found of thee.'

Isa. xxvi. 8.   'O Lord, we have waited for Thee : the desire of our soul is to Thy name.'

Isa. xxvi. 9.   'With my soul have I desired Thee in the night ; yea, with my spirit within me will I seek Thee early.'

Isa. lx. 19.   'The Lord shall be unto thee an everlasting light, and thy God thy glory.'

Sam. iii. 24, 25.   'The Lord is my portion, saith my soul ; therefore will I hope in Him. The Lord is good unto them that wait for Him, to the soul that seeketh Him.'

Psalm LXXXVII
(Seven Verses)

Verses

3, 5   These few verses point to the universality of the religion which emanates from Zion. 'Glorious things are spoken of thee, O city of

6, 7   God.' Of Zion it shall be said, 'This man was born there . . As well the singers as the players on instruments shall be there : all my springs are in Thee.'

PARALLEL VERSES

Isa. xii. 6   'Cry out and shout, thou inhabitant of Zion : for great is the Holy One of Israel in the midst of thee.'

'The Lord hath founded Zion, and the poor of His people shall Isa. xiv. 32.
trust in it.'

'The Lord is exalted ; for He dwelleth on high ; He hath filled Zion Isa. xxxiii. 5.
with judgment and righteousness.'

'   The people shall dwell in Zion at Jerusalem ; thou shalt Isa. xxx. 19.
weep no more.'

'   The ransomed of the Lord shall return, and come to Zion, Isa. xxxv. 10.
with songs and everlasting joy upon their heads : they shall obtain joy
and gladness, and sorrow and sighing shall flee away.'

'Awake, awake ; put on thy strength, O Zion ; put on thy beau- Isa. lii. 1.
tiful garments, O Jerusalem, the holy city.'

'   The Lord shall yet comfort you, and shall yet choose Zech. i. 17.
Jerusalem.'

Psalm LXXXVIII

(*Eighteen Verses*)

Verses

This Psalm is the lamentation of one 'whose soul is full of 3
troubles' sore and bitter. He had wept both day and night : ' Lord, 9
I have called daily upon Thee.' These prayers of anguish awakened 10
reflections such as these : ' Shall the dead arise and praise Thee, 11
or Thy lovingkindness be declared in the grave ? But unto Thee 13
have I cried, O Lord ; and in the morning shall my prayer prevent
Thee.'

Parallel Verses

'   I did mourn as a dove : mine eyes fail with looking upward : Isa. xxxviii. 14.
O Lord, I am oppressed ; undertake for me.'

Psalm LXXXIX

(*Fifty-two Verses*)

Verses

This Psalm presents a bright contrast to the mournful one which
precedes it. It is one of revival of spirit. ' I will sing of the 1, 2
mercies of the Lord for ever : with my mouth will I make known
Thy faithfulness to all generations.' The Psalmist praises God for

6 His wonderful power. 'For who in the heaven can be compared unto the Lord? who among the sons of the mighty can be likened
11 unto the Lord? The heavens are Thine, the earth also is Thine ; as for the world and the fulness thereof Thou hast founded them.
14 Justice and judgment are the habitation of Thy throne; mercy and
15 truth shall go before Thy face.' Blessed are those who walk in the
16 light of His countenance. 'In Thy name shall they rejoice all the
17, 18 day, for Thou art the glory of their strength ; the Lord is our defence ;
20 and the Holy One of Israel is our King.' God is represented as
29 speaking of David, whose seed shall endure for ever, and his throne
36, 37 as the days of heaven—'as the sun before Me. It shall be established for ever as the moon, and as a faithful witness in heaven.'
44 The Psalmist records with sorrow that his (David's) throne has been
46 'cast down to the ground,' and asks : 'How long, Lord? wilt Thou
47 hide thyself for ever ?' He contemplates the shortness of life—death is
48, 49 the mortal end of every human life, and none can deliver himself 'from the hand of the grave. Lord, where are Thy former lovingkindnesses,
51 which Thou swarest unto David in Thy truth?' The enemies of God 'have reproached the footsteps of Thine anointed.' The Psalmist says
52 finally : 'Blessed be the Lord for evermore. Amen, and Amen.'

Parallel Verses

Deut. xxxii. 3, 4.
'   I will publish the name of the Lord : ascribe ye greatness unto our God. He is the rock, His work is perfect : for all His ways are judgment : a God of truth, and without iniquity, just and right is He.'

1 Chron. xvi. 14.
'He is the Lord our God ; His judgments are in all the earth.'

Ecc. xii. 4.
'For God shall bring every work into judgment, with every secret thing, whether it be good, or whether it be evil.'

Isa. xxx. 18.
'And therefore will the Lord wait, that He may be gracious unto you, ... that He may have mercy upon you : for the Lord is a God of judgment.'

Isa. xlv. 21.
'Blessed are all they that wait for Him.   There is no God else beside Me ; a just God and a Saviour ; there is none beside Me.'

Psalm XC

(Seventeen Verses) Verses

This Psalm, headed ' A prayer of Moses, the man of God,' reflects upon man's relations with God, as far back as it is possible for human thought to carry us—from 'everlasting to everlasting.' 'Before the earth was formed Thou art God.' We are brought to God by means of suffering. This theory, that has been emphasised by all our teachers of old, solves many a difficult problem of life on earth. For a thousand years in God's sight are 'but as yesterday when it is past, as a watch in the night.' 'Our secret sins' are seen 'in the light' of His countenance. 'We spend our years as a tale that is told.' Taking into account the shortness of time allotted to us on earth, how urgent is it that we should 'number our days,' and apply our hearts to wisdom ! The years of man are about threescore and ten, and if 'by reason of strength they be fourscore years,' 'yet is their strength labour and sorrow ; for it is soon cut off, and we fly away.' The Psalmist prays that we may 'rejoice and be glad' in proportion to the days wherein we have been afflicted. He prays that the 'beauty of the Lord our God be upon us.'

2

3

4

8

9

12

14

17

PARALLEL VERSES

' Thou shalt consider in thine heart, that as a man chasteneth his son, so the Lord thy God chasteneth thee.' — Deut. viii. 5.

' Is there not an appointed time to man upon earth ? Are not his days also like the days of an hireling ? ' — Job vii. 1.

' He knoweth the way that I take : when he hath tried me, I shall come forth as gold.' — Job xxiii. 10.

' Behold, I have refined thee, but not with silver ; I have chosen thee in the furnace of affliction.' — Isa. xlviii. 10.

' And I will bring the third part through the fire, and will refine them as silver is refined, and I will try them as gold is tried : they shall call on My name, and I will hear them : I will say, It is My people, and they shall say, The Lord is my God.' — Zech. xiii. 9.

Psalm XCI

(*Sixteen Verses*)

Verses

1, 2	Here is described the blessed state of mind of those who live 'under the shadow of the Almighty,' my 'refuge,' my 'fortress' : 'my
4	God ; in Him will I trust . His truth shall be thy shield and
5	buckler.' Every source of fear will be dispelled : 'terror by night,' the
6	'arrow by day,' 'pestilence that walketh in darkness,' 'destruction that
10	wasteth at noonday ;' no 'evil,' nor 'shall any plague come nigh thy
11	dwelling.' For God will give 'His angels charge over thee, to keep
15, 16	thee in all thy ways.' 'He shall call upon Me, and I will answer him : I will be with him in trouble,' and 'with long life will I satisfy him.'

PARALLEL VERSES

2 Sam. xxii. 31.   'As for God, His way is perfect. The word of the Lord is tried · He is a buckler to all them that trust in Him.'

2 Sam. xxii. 33.   'God is my strength and power ; and He maketh my way perfect.'

1 Chron. xvi. 11.   'Seek the Lord and His strength, seek His face continually.'

Prov. xiv. 2.   'In the fear of the Lord is strong confidence ; and His children shall have a place of refuge.'

Prov. xviii. 10.   'The name of the Lord is a strong tower ; the righteous runneth unto it, and is safe.'

Psalm XCII

(*Fifteen Verses*)

Verses

1	'A Psalm or Song for the Sabbath day.' 'It is good to give thanks
2	unto the Lord, and to sing praises unto Thy name, O most High : to shew forth Thy lovingkindness' and 'faithfulness.' The Psalmist de-
5	scribes the peace and joy which are derived from the contemplation
6	of the works of God. The ungodly man does not 'understand this.'
13	'Those that be planted in the house of the Lord' shall still bring
14, 15	forth fruit in old age ; 'to shew that the Lord is upright : He is my rock, and there is no unrighteousness in Him.'

Those who avail themselves of the blessings of the Sabbath will understand the lovingkindness of God, and find their joy on that holy day.

PARALLEL VERSES

'And God blessed the seventh day, and sanctified it.' Gen. ii. 3.

'Remember the Sabbath day to keep it holy. Six days shalt thou Ex. xx. 8-10. labour and do all thy work'; but the seventh day is the Sabbath of the Lord thy God'; . . . . for 'thy son,' 'thy daughter,' 'thy household,' and 'thy stranger that is within thy gates.'

'Blessed is the man . . . . that keepeth the Sabbath, ... and Isa. lvi. 2. keepeth his hand from evil.'

'   If (thou) call the Sabbath a delight, the holy of the Lord, Isa. lviii. 13,14. honourable ; and shalt honour Him, not doing thine own ways nor finding thine own pleasure : . . . . then shalt thou delight thyself in the Lord.   The mouth of the Lord hath spoken it.'

Psalm XCIII

(*Five Verses*)   Verses

In this short poem the Psalmist pours out his adoration, describing the holiness and power of God. 'The Lord reigneth,' 'clothed with   1 majesty' and 'strength ;   Thou art from everlasting. . . . The   2, 4 Lord on high is mightier than the noise of many waters, yea, than the mighty waves of the sea. . . . Holiness becometh Thine house, O   5 Lord, for ever.'

PARALLEL VERSES

'Behold, the heaven and the heaven of heavens is the Lord's thy Deut. x. 14. God, the earth also, with all that therein is.'

'Glory and honour are in His presence ; strength and gladness are 1 Chron. xvi. in His place.'   27.

'Give unto the Lord, ye kindreds of the people, give unto the Lord 1 Chron. xvi. glory and strength.'   28.

'Give unto the Lord the glory due unto His name : . . . . worship 1 Chron. xvi· the Lord in the beauty of holiness.'   29.

Psalm XCIV

(Twenty-three Verses)

4
5
7
8

The Psalmist utters a severe denunciation against the 'workers of iniquity.' 'They break in pieces Thy people, O Lord, and afflict Thine heritage. . . . They say, The Lord shall not see.' Thus the Psalmist describes the 'brutish among the people.'

9, 10
11
12
14

The writer then reflects upon the omniscience of God. 'He that planted the ear, shall He not hear? He that formed the eye, shall He not see? . . . The Lord knoweth the thoughts of man.' Blessed is the man whom God corrects, and 'teaches out of Thy law. . . . For the Lord will not cast off His people, neither will He forsake His inheritance.'

17
18

The following verses are gems of spiritual religion ; they express the deepest truths of human experience: 'Unless the Lord had been my help, my soul had almost dwelt in silence. When I said, My foot slippeth ; Thy mercy, O Lord, held me up.'

19
22

'In the multitude of my thoughts within me Thy comforts delight my soul. . . . The Lord is my defence ; and my God is the rock of my refuge.'

PARALLEL VERSES

Deut. iv. 31.

'. . . . (The Lord thy God is a merciful God ;) He will not forsake thee, neither destroy thee, nor forget the covenant of thy fathers which He sware unto thee.'

Job v. 12.

'He disappointeth the devices of the crafty, so that their hands cannot perform their enterprises.'

Job x. 4.

'Hast thou eyes of flesh? or seest thou as man seeth?'

Job xxxiii. 12.

'   God is greater than man.'

Prov. xxix. 2.

'When the righteous are in authority, the people rejoice : but when the wicked beareth rule, the people mourn.'

Psalm XCV

(Eleven Verses)

3

This is a joyous hymn of praise. The Psalmist says : 'O come, let us sing unto the Lord: let us make a joyful noise to the rock of our salvation. . . . The Lord is a great God.'   The sea and the dry land are   5

His.   'O come, let us worship and bow down : let us kneel before the   6

Lord our maker.   For He is our God ; and we are the people of His   7

pasture, and the sheep of His hand.'

PARALLEL VERSES

'And they entered into a covenant to seek the Lord God of their   2 Chron. xv.

fathers, with all their heart, and with all their soul.'   12.

'And they sware unto the Lord with a loud voice, and with shout-   2 Chron. xv.

ing, and with trumpets, and with cornets.'   14.

'   And sought Him with their whole desire ; and He was   2 Chron. xv.

found of them : and the Lord gave them rest round about.'   15.

Psalm XCVI

(*Thirteen Verses*)   Verses

The same subject continued—a joyous hymn of praise and worship.

'For the Lord is great, and greatly to be praised. . . . The Lord made   4, 5

the heavens. . . . Honour and majesty, ... strength and beauty are in   6

His sanctuary. . . . . O worship the Lord in the beauty of holiness : fear   9

before Him, all the earth. . . . He shall judge the people righteously.'   10

All nature is called upon to be joyful—the 'heavens,' the 'earth,'   11

the 'sea,' the 'field,' and the 'trees of the wood' shall *all* 'rejoice

before the Lord' : for He will judge the 'earth,' and the world with   13

'righteousness,' and the people with His 'truth.'

PARALLEL VERSES

'. . . . Ye shall rejoice in all that ye put your hand unto, ye and   Deut. xii. 7.

your households, wherein the Lord thy God hath blessed thee.'

'My heart rejoiceth in the Lord.'   1 Sam. ii. 1.

'Sing unto the Lord, all the earth.'   1 Chron. xvi.

    23.

'Declare His glory among the heathen ; His marvellous works   1 Chron. xvi.

among all nations.'   24.

'Fear before Him, all the earth ; the world also.'   1 Chron. xvi.

    30.

'Let the heavens be glad, and let the earth rejoice : and let men   1 Chron. xvi.

say among the nations, The Lord reigneth,' &c.   31.

Psalm XCVII

(Twelve Verses)

Another hymn exhorting all nature to join in the worship of
God alone.   The Psalmist condemns the worship of idols, and those
who serve graven images.   'Zion heard, and was glad : and the
daughters of Judah rejoiced because of Thy judgments, O Lord.'
Those who love God 'hate evil.'   'Light is sown for the righteous, and
gladness for the upright in heart.   Rejoice in the Lord, ye righteous ;
and give thanks at the remembrance of His holiness.'

Verses: 7, 8, 10, 11, 12

PARALLEL VERSES

Isa. xlii. 10.   'Sing unto the Lord a new song, and His praise from the end of the
earth, ye that go down to the sea, and all that is therein ; the isles, and
the inhabitants thereof.'

Isa. xlii. 11.   '   . Let the inhabitants of the rock sing, let them shout from the
top of the mountains.'

Isa. xlii. 12.   'Let them give glory unto the Lord, and declare His praise in the
islands.'

Dan. ii. 19.   '   Then Daniel blessed the God of heaven.   Daniel
Dan. ii. 20.   said, Blessed be the name of God for ever and ever : for wisdom and
might are His.'

Psalm XCVIII

(Nine Verses)

Verses

This is again a song of joyous praise, beginning with the words of
Isaiah xlii. 10 : 'O sing unto the Lord a new song.'   The Psalm
continues : 'He hath remembered His mercy and His truth toward the
house of Israel. . . . Let the hills be joyful together before the Lord ;
for He cometh to judge the earth : with righteousness shall He judge
the world, and the people with equity.'

Verses: 1, 3, 8, 9

PARALLEL VERSES

Deut. xxxii. 4.   'He is the Rock, His work is perfect : for all His ways are
judgment : a God of truth and without iniquity, just and right is He.'

Shall any teach God knowledge, seeing that He judgeth those that   Job xxi. 22.
are high ?'

'Touching the Almighty, we cannot find Him out: He is excellent   Job xxxvii. 23.
in power, and in judgment, and in plenty of justice; He will not
afflict.   He respecteth not any that are wise of heart.'   Job xxxvii. 24.

Psalm XCIX

(*Nine Verses*)

Verses

The Psalmist continues to sing praise to the Almighty : 'The Lord   2
reigneth. . . . The Lord is great in Zion; and He is high above all
people.' The Psalmist looks back upon Israel's history. 'Moses and   6
Aaron were among His priests, and Samuel among them that call upon
His name ; they called upon the Lord, and He answered them.
Worship at His footstool; for He is holy. . . . Exalt the Lord our   9
God, and worship at His holy hill; for the Lord our God is holy.'

PARALLEL VERSES

'   Moses stood in the gate of the camp, and said, Who is on   Ex. xxxii. 26.
the Lord's side? let him come unto me; and all the sons of Levi
gathered themselves together unto him.   '

'And the children of Levi did according to the word of Moses :   Ex. xxxii. 28.
and the Lord spake unto Moses, saying : . . . . Phineas, the son of   Num. xxv. 10.
Eleazar, the son of Aaron the priest . . . . was zealous for My sake.'   Num. xxv. 11.

'Wherefore say, Behold I give unto him My covenant of peace :   Num. xxv. 12.
and he shall have it, and his seed after him, even the covenant of an   Num. xxv. 13.
everlasting priesthood ; because he was zealous for his God. .   '

'And it shall come to pass . . . . that the mountain of the Lord's   Isa. ii. 2.
house shall be established in the top of the mountains, and shall be
exalted above the hills.   '

'And many people shall go up to the mountain of the Lord, to   Isa. ii. 3.
the house of the God of Jacob ; and He will teach us of His ways,
and we will walk in His paths : for out of Zion shall go forth the law,
and the word of the Lord from Jerusalem.'

Psalm C

(*Five Verses*)

3

4

5

In this universal 'Psalm of praise,' all 'lands' are exhorted to unite in a chorus of joyful song, 'the Lord He is God,' and 'He hath made us, and not we ourselves'; therefore must we 'enter into His gates with thanksgiving and praise. . . . For the Lord is good; His mercy is everlasting; and His truth endureth to all generations.'

PARALLEL VERSES

1 Chron. xvi. 31.

'Let the heavens be glad, and let the earth rejoice : and let men say among the nations, The Lord reigneth.'

1 Chron. xvi. 32.

'. . . . Let the fields rejoice, and all that is therein.'

1 Chron. xvi. 33.

'Then shall the trees of the wood sing out, at the presence of the Lord. . . .'

1 Chron. xvi. 34.

'O give thanks unto the Lord ; for He is good : for His mercy endureth for ever.'

Psalm CI

(*Eight Verses*)

~

6

7

8

The Psalmist declares that he will behave 'wisely in a perfect way,' and walk within his house with a 'perfect heart.' He resolves to search for the faithful of the land, that they may serve him. He hates falsehood and deceit ; and resolves to remove all 'wicked doers' from the 'city of the Lord.'

PARALLEL VERSES

Lev. xix. 2.

'. . . . Ye shall be holy : for I the Lord your God am holy.'

Deut. xviii. 13.

'Thou shalt be perfect with the Lord thy God.'

2 Chron. xix. 9.

'And he (King of Judah) charged them, saying, Thus shall ye do in the fear of the Lord, faithfully, and with a perfect heart.'

Prov. ii. 20.

'   . That thou mayest walk in the way of good men and keep the paths of the righteous.'

Prov. ii. 21.

'For the upright shall dwell in the land, and the perfect shall remain in it.'

Psalm CII

(*Twenty-eight Verses*)

This Psalm is an outpouring of the soul in a time of overwhelming affliction and personal suffering. 'Hide not Thy face from me in the day when I am in trouble ; incline Thine ear unto me : in the day when I call answer me speedily.' The Psalmist says that his 'heart is smitten,' so that he forgets to take his food ; his days are 'like a shadow that declineth,' and withered like grass ; . . . . but God shall endure for ever. He comforts himself in his faith and in the belief that God will not despise the prayer of the destitute. 'This shall be written for the generation to come.' God looks down from heaven. He hears the groaning of the prisoner. God's name shall be proclaimed in Zion, and His praise in Jerusalem. The people shall be gathered together, and the 'kingdoms to serve the Lord.' The Psalmist's strength was weakened, his days were cut short. Thus he prayed, 'O my God, take me not away in the midst of my days · Thy years are throughout all generations.' The earth and the heavens are the work of God's hands. They may perish, but God shall endure for ever. God's years 'have no end.' The children of His people shall continue, and their seed shall be established before God.

	Verses
	2
	4
	11
	12
	16
	17
	18
	19, 20
	21
	22
	23
	24
	25
	26
	28

PARALLEL VERSES

'My soul is weary of my life : I will speak in the bitterness of my soul.'   Job x. 1.

'. . . . My friends scorn me : but mine eye poureth out tears unto God.'   Job xvi. 20.

'My members are as a shadow.'   Job xvii. 7.

'. . . . Mine eyes fail with looking upward : O Lord, I am oppressed ; undertake for me.'   Isa. xxxviii. 14.

'O Lord, behold my affliction.'   Lam. i. 9.

'Behold, O Lord ; for I am in distress, mine heart is turned within me.'   Lam. i. 20.

' . . For my sighs are many, and my heart is faint.'   Lam. i. 22.

Habak. iii. 2.   ' O Lord, revive Thy work ; in wrath remember mercy.'

Nahum i. 7.   'The Lord is good, a strong hold in the day of trouble.'

2 Kings xx. 5.   ' I have heard thy prayer, I have seen thy tears.'

Psalm CIII

(*Twenty-two Verses*)

\erses

3, 4, 5   In this utterance of the soul's recognition of God, the Psalmist
13   makes a summary, as it were, of the Almighty's infinite love in
14   relation to man.   'Like as a father pitieth his children, so the
          Lord pitieth them that fear Him.   For He knoweth our frame ; He
          remembereth that we are dust.'   The Psalmist likens the days of man
15   to the 'grass,' and the 'flower of the field,' whereas the 'mercy of
          God' is from 'everlasting to everlasting,' as seen in the generations of
20   those whose lives have been godly ; such are God's angels in heaven,
          ' hearkening unto the voice of His word.'   He concludes his reflections
          as he began : ' Bless the Lord, O my soul.'

PARALLEL VERSES

Isa. xl. 6.   ' All flesh is grass, and all the goodliness thereof is as the flower of
the field.'

Isa. xl. 7.   ' . . . . The grass withereth, the flower fadeth : because the Spirit
of the Lord bloweth upon it.'

Isa. xl. 8.   ' . . . . The grass withereth, the flower fadeth : but the word of
our God shall stand for ever.'

Ecc. xii. 7.   ' Then shall the dust return to the earth as it was : and the spirit
shall return unto God who gave it.'

Isa. lxiv. 4.   Since the beginning of the world men have not heard,
nor perceived by the ear, neither hath the eye seen, O God, beside
Thee, what He hath prepared for him that waiteth for Him.'

Prov. xii. 28.   ' In the way of righteousness is life ; and in the pathway thereof
there is no death.'

Psalm CIV

(*Thirty-five Verses*)

This noble Psalm describes the power and the Spirit of God
as manifested throughout all creation : ' Thou art very great.' In
poetic language the Psalmist describes God—clothed 'with light as
with a garment,' the 'clouds His chariot'; walking upon the 'wings
of the wind,' His 'angels spirits'; all creation obeying His will;
causing the 'grass to grow for the cattle,' 'herbs for the service of
man'; 'wine' and bread that give strength to man ; the moon that
marks times and seasons. 'The sun knoweth his going down.' The
sun rises, and ' man goeth forth unto his work and to his labour until
the evening.' He exclaims : ' O Lord, how manifold are Thy works !
in wisdom hast Thou made them all ; the earth is full of Thy riches,'
so is the great and wide sea. When God hides His face from us we
are troubled. 'The glory of the Lord shall endure for ever.' With
these meditations the Psalmist declares that he will sing praises to God
as long as he lives. He desires that the wicked shall be no more. ' Bless
the Lord, O my soul. Praise ye the Lord.'

1
2
3
4
14
15
19
23
24

25
29, 31

33
35

PARALLEL VERSES

' In the beginning God created the heaven and the earth. And the
earth was without form, and void ; and darkness was upon the face of
the deep. And the Spirit of God moved upon the face of the waters.' Gen. i. 1, 2.

' And God said, Let there be light ; and there was light.' Gen. i. 3.

' He hath made the earth by His power, He hath established the
world by His wisdom, and hath stretched out the heavens by His
discretion.' Jer. x. 12.

' He that tilleth his land shall be satisfied with bread.' Prov. xii. 11.

' The soul of the sluggard desireth and hath nothing : but the soul
of the diligent shall be made fat.' Prov. xiii. 4.

' He that followeth after righteousness and mercy findeth life,
righteousness, and honour.' Prov. xxi. 21.

Psalm CV

(Forty-five Verses)

This is the Psalm which David delivered, as recorded in 1 Chron. xvi. It is a declaration of thanksgiving to God for His marvellous deeds to the children of Israel, to whom the Psalmist appeals in these words : 'O ye seed of Abraham, his servant, ye children of Jacob His chosen. He is the Lord our God : His judgments are in all the earth.' The Psalmist recounts the history of the covenant which God made with Abraham, confirmed the same to Jacob for a law, an 'everlasting covenant,' saying, 'Unto thee will I give the land of Canaan, the lot of your inheritance.' From verse 12 to verse 37 he gives a summary of the history of Israel in Egypt. 'Egypt was glad when they departed : for the fear of them fell upon them'; a cloud had led them by day, and 'fire to give light in the night.' God 'remembered His holy promise, and Abraham His servant.' 'He brought forth His people with joy, ... that they might observe His statutes, and keep His laws. Praise ye the Lord.'

Verse markers in left margin: 6, 7, 9, 10, 11, 38, 39, 42, 43, 45

PARALLEL VERSES

1 Sam. xii. 24. 'Only fear the Lord and serve Him in truth with all your heart : for consider how great things He hath done for you.'

Isaiah xlix. 13. 'Sing, O heavens ; and be joyful, O earth ; and break forth into singing, O mountains : for the Lord hath comforted His people, and will have mercy upon His afflicted.'

Isaiah li. 4. 'Hearken unto Me, My people ; and give ear unto Me, O My nation : for a law shall proceed from Me, and I will make My judgment to rest for a light of the people.'

Nehemiah viii. 6. 'And Ezra blessed the Lord, the great God. And all the people answered, Amen, Amen, with lifting up their hands : and they bowed their heads, and worshipped the Lord with their faces to the ground.'

Psalm CVI

(*Forty-eight Verses*)

This Psalm continues the subject of the previous one. 'Praise ye the Lord ; for He is good ; for His mercy endureth for ever.' In this epitome of the history of the children of Israel is described the genius of the religion which is their 'inheritance.' Great and sore have been their sufferings—the penalties of disobedience. They angered Moses and provoked his spirit, so that he 'spake unadvisedly with his lips.' They envied Moses in the camp and Aaron the saint of the Lord. They readily fell under the influence of their surroundings, and changed their glory to the worship of idols, and 'forgat God their Saviour which had done great things in Egypt. . . . Therefore was the wrath of the Lord kindled against His people, ... His own inheritance. . . . Nevertheless He regarded their affliction, when He heard their cry ; . . . according to the multitude of His mercies. He made them also to be pitied of all those that carried them captives.' The Psalmist concludes with a prayer and praise. 'Save us, O Lord our God, and gather us from among the heathen, to give thanks unto Thy holy name, and to triumph in Thy praise. Blessed be the Lord God of Israel from everlasting to everlasting : and let all the people say, Amen. Praise ye the Lord.'

1

5

32, 33
16

20, 21
40

44

45

46

47, 48

Parallel Verses

'And when the people complained, it displeased the Lord ; and the Lord heard it ; and His anger was kindled ; and the fire of the Lord burnt among them, and consumed them that were in the uttermost parts of the camp.' Num. xi. 1.

'And the people cried unto Moses ; and when Moses prayed unto the Lord, the fire was quenched.' Num. 2.

'Now the man Moses was very meek, above all the men which were upon the face of the earth.' Num. xii. 3.

(Moses said to his servant Joshua, the son of Nun,) 'Would God that all the Lord's people were prophets, and that the Lord would put His Spirit upon them !' Num. xi. 28.

Num. xiv. 11.   'The Lord said unto Moses, How long will this people provoke Me? and how long will it be ere they believe Me for all the signs which I have shewed among them?'

Read verses 17, 18, 19, 20, 22, 23, 24.   (After the prayer of Moses and his faith in God, the Lord said v. 20,) 'I have pardoned according to thy word.'

Psalm CVII

Verses

(*Forty-three Verses*)

The same subject continued, commencing : 'O give thanks unto the Lord, for He is good : for His mercy endureth for ever.' This is a beautiful poem. After intervals of reflection concerning Israel's 8, 15, 21, 31 history, the Psalmist exclaims : 'Oh that men would praise the Lord for His goodness, and for His wonderful works to the children of men !' Whilst recounting the events of Israel's history the Psalmist repeatedly exhorts men to praise the Lord for His goodness. He sets forth the marvellous manner in which God leads His people safely through the wilderness. They find help in the midst of their 13 sufferings. 'Then they cried unto the Lord in their trouble, and He saved them out of their distresses.' 'They that go down to the sea in ships, that do business in great waters' witness God's marvels 23, 29, 39 alike in the 'storm' and in the 'calm.' Although man suffers from 40, 41 'oppression,' 'affliction,' and 'sorrow,' God can pour 'contempt upon 42 princes, and raise up the poor on high.' The righteous shall see it and rejoice, and 'iniquity' be silenced. Finally the Psalmist exclaims, 43 Whoso is wise, and will observe these things, even they shall understand the lovingkindness of the Lord.'

PARALLEL VERSES

Deut. xxxiii. 27.   'The eternal God is thy refuge, and underneath are the everlasting arms.'

Deut. iv. 5.   'I have taught you statutes and judgments ; . . . . keep therefore Deut. iv. 6. and do them, for this is your wisdom and your understanding, in the sight of the nations, which shall hear all these statutes, and say, Surely this great nation is a wise and understanding people.'

Job v. 17.   '. . . . Happy is the man whom God correcteth ; therefore despise not thou the chastening of the Almighty; for He maketh sore and bindeth up; He woundeth, and His hands make whole. He shall deliver thee in six troubles; yea, in seven there shall no evil touch thee.' Job v. 18.
Job v. 19.

Psalm CVIII

(*Thirteen Verses*)

Verses

This is a hymn of joyous praise. The first five verses are identical with the last five verses of the 57th Psalm : '   O God, my heart is fixed : I will sing and give praise, even with my glory. Awake, psaltery and harp : I myself will awake early.   Give us help from trouble : for vain is the help of man. Through God we shall do valiantly, for He it is that shall tread down our enemies.' 1
2
13

PARALLEL VERSES

'The living, the living, he shall praise Thee, as I do this day.' Isa. xxxviii. 10.

'Let them give glory unto the Lord, and declare His praise in the islands.' Isa. xlii. 12.

'Blessed be the name of God for ever and ever : for wisdom and might are His.' Dan. ii. 20.

'The Lord is my rock, and my fortress, and my deliverer.' 2 Sam. xxii. 2.

'The God of my rock : in Him will I trust.' 2 Sam. xxii. 3.

Psalm CIX

(*Thirty-one Verses*)

This Psalm cannot be regarded as anything but a blot upon the Psalter. It is omitted from the Liturgy of the Synagogue. It is the outburst of one whose moral sense must have been temporarily clouded under the pressure of severe personal injustice.

Psalm CX

(*Seven Verses*)

This somewhat obscure Psalm refers to Israel's history from fragmentary records. Reference is made to the priestly order of

Melchizedek. 'The Lord shall send the rod of thy strength out of Zion.' 'The Lord hath sworn, and will not repent, Thou art a priest for ever after the order of Melchizedek.'

NOTE.—One parallel verse will suffice to illustrate the Psalmist's allusion to the fragmentary records of Israel's earliest history, described (v. 3) in poetic language as the 'beauties of holiness,' the 'dew of thy youth.'

We read in the 14th chapter of Genesis (the 18th verse) that Melchizedek, king of Salem, brought forth bread and wine, and he was the 'priest of the most high God'; and he blessed Abraham in these words:

19   'Blessed be Abram of the most high God, possessor of heaven and
20   earth, and blessed be the most high God.' The king of Salem said to
21, 23 Abraham, 'Take the goods to thyself.' Abraham replied, 'I will not take anything that is thine, lest thou shouldst say, I have made Abram rich.'

Psalm CXI

(*Ten Verses*)

Verses

1   The Psalmist praises God with his 'whole heart   in the assembly
2   of the upright.'[1]   God's works are 'great,' 'honourable,' and 'glorious.'
3, 4   His righteousness endureth for ever—'gracious' and 'full of compas-
5, 7   sion,' ever 'mindful of His covenant.' His works are 'verity' and
8   'judgment'; they 'stand fast for ever and ever' in truth and upright-
9   ness. 'Holy is His name.' The Psalmist exclaims: 'The fear of the
10   Lord is the beginning of wisdom: a good understanding have all they that do His commandments.'

[1] 'IN CONCILIO JUSTORUM' (Psalm cxi. 1).—'I will praise the Lord,' &c., 'in the assembly of the upright.' This was the motto selected by my beloved husband for the Serjeant's gold ring when he took the coif on February 11, 1864. These rings were presented to the Queen (a certain weight of gold), then to the judges and to private friends (an ancient custom). The order of the Serjeant existed from the twelfth century.

'Only fear the Lord and serve Him in truth with all your heart : for 1 Sam. xii. 24. consider how great things He hath done for you.'

'Therefore I will give thanks unto thee, O Lord, among the heathen, 2 Sam. xxii. 50. and I will sing praises unto Thy name.'

Psalm CXII

(*Ten Verses*)

Verses

Continuing his praises to God, the Psalmist describes the blessed-ness of the godly man. His seed shall possess powerful influence upon   2 earth. The generation of the upright shall be blessed. His righteous-   3, 4 ness endureth for ever. Unto the upright light ariseth in darkness ; for   5 he is gracious, full of compassion, and righteous. He will guide his   6 affairs with discretion, and he shall be in 'everlasting remembrance.'   7 His heart is fixed, trusting in the Lord. He has given to the poor.   9 'His horn shall be exalted with honour.' The Psalmist contrasts the   10 godly with the ungodly man.

'Whoso trusteth in the Lord, happy is he.'   Prov. xvi. 20.

'The name of the Lord is a strong tower : the righteous runneth Prov. xviii. 10. into it, and is safe.'

'Who is among you that feareth the Lord, that obeyeth the voice of Isa. l. 10. His servant, that walketh in darkness, and hath no light? Let him trust in the name of the Lord, and stay upon his God.'

'The hope of the righteous shall be gladness.'   Prov. x. 28.

'He that followeth after righteousness and mercy findeth life, right- Prov. xxi. 21. eousness, and honour.'

Psalm CXIII

(*Nine Verses*)

Verses

Here are further praises to God : ' From the rising of the   3 sun unto the going down of the same, the Lord's name is to be praised. . . . Who is like unto the Lord our God?' Although He dwells   5 on high, He beholds the things on earth as He does in heaven. 'He

Verses
7
9

raiseth up the poor out of the dust, and lifteth the needy out of the dunghill ; that he may be seated with princes.' ' Praise ye the Lord.'

PARALLEL VERSES

Lam. iii. 41.

'Let us lift up our hearts with our hands unto God in the heavens.'

Lam. iii. 49.

'Mine eye trickleth down, and ceaseth not, without any inter- mission.'

Lam. iii. 50.

'Till the Lord look down, and behold from heaven.'

Micah vii. 8.

' When I fall, I shall arise ; when I sit in darkness, the Lord shall be a light unto me.'

Psalm CXIV
(*Eight Verses*)

Verses

1

3

7

Alluding to the exodus from Egypt, the Psalmist proclaims the glory of God in poetical language : ' The sea saw it and fled ·   the moun- tains skipped like rams, and the little hills like lambs. . . . Tremble, thou earth, at the presence of the Lord, at the presence of the God of Jacob.'

PARALLEL VERSES

Ex. xv. 10.

' Thou didst blow with Thy wind, the sea covered them : they sank as lead in the mighty waters.'

Ex. xv. 11.

'Who is like unto Thee, O Lord, among the gods? who is like Thee, glorious in holiness, fearful in praises, doing wonders ? '

Ex. xv. 17.

'Thou shalt bring them in, and plant them in the mountain of Thine inheritance, in the place, O Lord, which Thou hast made for Thee to dwell in, in the sanctuary, O Lord.'

Ex. xv. 18.

' The Lord shall reign for ever and ever.'

Psalm CXV
(*Eighteen Verses*)

Verse

1

The Psalmist gives expression to the contrast between the wor- ship of idols and the worship of God : 'Not unto us, O Lord, not unto us, but unto Thy name give glory, for Thy mercy and for

Thy truth's sake.' This Psalm is almost word for word the same as the 135th Psalm. Both contain an indignant protest against the makers of idols—' their idols of silver and gold, the work of   4 men's hands.' They have ' eyes ' and ' mouths ' and ' ears,' but can   5 neither see, hear, or speak. 'They that make them are like unto   8 them : so is every one that trusteth in them ' (see Ps. 135, verses 15, 16, 17, 18). The Psalmist appeals to the house of Israel, to the priestly tribe of Aaron and Levi, to take warning against idolatry, for ' ye are   15 blessed of the Lord, which made heaven and earth. The heaven, even   16 the heavens, are the Lord's : but the earth hath He given to the children of men.' It is in our lives that we must 'praise the Lord from this   18 time forth and for evermore.'

PARALLEL VERSES

' And Solomon stood before the altar of the Lord in the presence of   1 Kings viii. 22. all the congregation of Israel, and spread forth his hands toward heaven, and he said, Lord God of Israel, there is no God like Thee,   1 Kings viii. 23. in heaven above, or on earth beneath. . . .'

' But will God indeed dwell on the earth ? behold, the heaven and   1 Kings viii. 27. heaven of heavens cannot contain Thee ; how much less this house that I have builded ? '

' . . . When Solomon had made an end of praying, ... from   1 Kings viii. 54. kneeling on his knees, with his hands spread up to heaven,   . . he   1 Kings viii. 55. stood and blessed all the congregation of Israel. . . '

'That all the people of the earth may know that the Lord is God,   1 Kings viii. 60. and that there is none else.'

Psalm CXVI

(Nineteen Verses)

The Psalmist declares his love to God, because his prayers have   2 been heard, 'therefore will I call upon Him as long as I live.' He has experienced deliverance from great and sore trouble ; he 'was   6 brought low,' and God helped him.

' Return unto thy rest, O my soul ; for the Lord hath dealt bountifully   7, 8 with thee.' ' Precious in the sight of the Lord is the death of His saints.'   15

He had been greatly afflicted, and in his haste he exclaimed, 'All men are liars.' Now he is overflowing with gratitude. 'I will walk before the Lord in the land of the living. . . . I will pay my vows . . . in the courts of the Lord's house, in the midst of thee, O Jerusalem. Praise ye the Lord.'

PARALLEL VERSES

2 Sam. xxii. 1.   'And David spake unto the Lord the words of this song in the day that the Lord had delivered him out of the hand of his enemies, and out of the hand of Saul : '

2 Sam. xxii. 4.   'I will call upon the Lord, who is worthy to be praised : so shall I be saved from mine enemies.'

2 Sam. xxii. 5.   'When the waves of death compassed me, the floods of ungodly men made me afraid.'

2 Sam. xxii. 6.   'The sorrows of hell compassed me about : the snares of death prevented me.'

2 Sam. xxii. 7.   'In my distress I called upon the Lord, and cried to my God : and He did hear my voice out of His temple, and my cry did enter into His ears.'

2 Sam. xxii. 17.   'He sent from above, He took me ; He drew me out of many waters.'

2 Sam. xxii. 19.   '   The Lord was my stay.'

Psalm CXVII

(*Two Verses*)

This brief Psalm belongs to the group of hymns of praise in which all nations and all people are exhorted to praise the Lord. 'For His merciful kindness is great towards us ; and the truth of the Lord endureth for ever. Praise ye the Lord.'

PARALLEL VERSES

1 Chron. xvi. 28.   'Give unto the Lord, ye kindreds of the people, give unto the Lord
1 Chron. xvi. 29.   glory and strength ; give unto the Lord the glory due unto His name.'
Isa. lxvi. 5.   '   Let the Lord be glorified.'
Hab. iii. 3.   '. . . . His glory covered the heavens, and the earth was full of His praise.'

Psalm CXVIII

(*Twenty-nine Verses*)

The Psalmist exhorts all people to 'give thanks unto the Lord ; for   1
He is good : because His mercy endureth for ever.'   He appeals to
Israel, to the house of Aaron, and to all who fear God, to say that
His 'mercy endureth for ever.'   Referring to his personal experiences, when in distress he called upon God.   The Lord answered   5
him ; therefore, he says, it is better to trust in the Lord than to put   8
confidence in man or in princes.   The enemy thrust sore at him,   9, 13
that he might fall ; but the Lord helped him.   The Lord is his strength   14
and his song, and his salvation.   He declares that although he has
been sorely tried, he will yet live to declare the works of God,   18
praying that the gates of righteousness may be open to him, that he   19
may enter them, and praise the Lord.   The day of rejoicing has   24
come to him ; he prays now for prosperity.   God is the Lord which has   25, 27
shown him light.   'Thou art my God, and I will praise Thee.'   He   28
ends as he began : 'O give thanks unto the Lord ; for He is good : for   29
His mercy endureth for ever.'

PARALLEL VERSES

'The Lord liveth : and blessed be my rock ; and exalted be the   2 Sam. xxii. 47.
God of the rock of my salvation.'

'It is God that avengeth me, and that bringeth down the people   2 Sam. xxii. 48.
under me, and that bringeth me forth from mine enemies.   Thou hast   2 Sam. xxii. 49.
also lifted me up on high above those that rose up against me.   Thou
hast delivered me from the violent man.'

'Therefore I will give thanks unto Thee, O Lord, among the   2 Sam. xxii. 50.
heathen, and I will sing praises unto Thy name.'

' He is the tower of salvation for His king, and sheweth mercy unto   2 Sam. xxii. 51.
His anointed, unto David, and to his seed for evermore.'

Psalm CXIX

(*One hundred and seventy-six Verses*)

This is the alphabetical Psalm. It is divided into twenty-two parts of eight verses. Every verse in each part commences with the same letter repeated eight times, thus giving the twenty-two letters of the Hebrew alphabet in complete order. The Psalmist gives expression to a series of devotional exercises for reflection and prayer, through every vicissitude of mortal life. The laws of God are the basis of the reflections.

SUMMARY

Aleph 1-8.
Blessed are those who walk in the law of the Lord, who seek Him with the whole heart; none who do so shall have cause for shame.

Beth 9-16.
The only shelter from sin is in the firm resolve to find pleasure in God's laws. 'I will . . . . have respect unto Thy ways. . . . I will not forget Thy word.'

Gimel 17-24.
The Psalmist prays to God that he may live, in order to comprehend the wonders of God's commandments.

Daleth 25-32.
He knows that human resolves for good may fail us unless quickened by means of direct communion with God; therefore he prays, 'Teach

He 33-40.
me, O Lord, the way of Thy statutes,' 'give me understanding, and I shall keep Thy law; yea, I shall observe it with my whole heart.' 'Turn away mine eyes from beholding vanity, and quicken Thou me in Thy way.'

Vau 41-48.
He also prays for mercy, that he may be able to walk at liberty, without the fear of shame; that he may speak of God's testimonies in the presence of kings.

Zain 49-56.
The Psalmist has cause to hope in the word of God, which has been his comfort in affliction, although he was derided by the proud. He felt horror in the presence of the wicked. In the night he found comfort in thoughts about God.

Cheth 57-64.
The Psalmist declares himself to be a companion of all those who seek God and keep His precepts. 'Thou art my portion, O Lord. . . . Be merciful unto me, according to Thy word. At midnight

I will rise to give thanks unto Thee because of Thy righteous judgments,' for the earth 'is full of Thy mercy.'

The discipline of affliction is then dwelt upon. Before he was Teth 65-72. afflicted he went astray. 'It is good for me that I have been afflicted.' He puts a higher value upon the laws of God than upon thousands of gold and silver.

Meditating upon the judgments and faithfulness of God, he says it Jod 73-80. was God who formed him. To God he prays for 'understanding.' 'I know, O Lord, that Thy judgments are right.' He has been comforted in God's tender mercies, and prays, 'Let my heart be sound in Thy statutes ; that I be not ashamed.'

The Psalmist reflects on the shortness of life, and asks, 'How Caph 81-88. many are the days of Thy servant?' He complains bitterly of his persecutors, but his faith has not failed him. 'Help Thou me.' 'Quicken me after Thy lovingkindness.'

'For ever, O Lord, Thy word is settled in heaven. . . . Unless Thy Lamed 89-96. law had been my delights, I should then have perished in mine affliction.' Never can he forget God's precepts, for 'with them Thou hast quickened me. I am Thine.'

The Psalmist exclaims, 'O how love I Thy law ! It is my medita- Mem 97-104. tion all the day.' Through these studies he obtains more wisdom and understanding than his enemies, and he has been enabled to 'refrain' his feet 'from every evil way.' God's words are 'sweeter to his taste than honey.' Hence it is that he hates 'every false way.'

The word of God is a lamp to his feet and a light on his path. Nun 105-112.

Again the Psalmist refers to his afflictions. He prays God to accept the freewill offerings of his mouth ; he has sworn obedience to God's law. 'Thy testimonies have I taken as an heritage for ever.' They are 'the rejoicings of my heart.'

'I hate vain thoughts ; but Thy law do I love. Thou art my hiding Samech 113-120. place and my shield : I hope in Thy word. . . . Uphold me that I may live : and let me not be ashamed of my hope. Hold Thou me up, and I shall be safe.'

The Psalmist prays : 'Leave me not to my oppressors. . . . Deal Ain 121-128. with Thy servant according to Thy mercy. I love Thy commandments above gold. . . . I hate every false way.'

Pe 129–136.　　　　He declares that the words of God give both 'light' and 'under-standing'—even to the 'simple'; therefore his soul 'doth keep them.' He prays to God to look upon him with the mercy that was shown to those who loved His name, and that iniquity may not have dominion over him. 'Make Thy face to shine upon Thy servant.' Tears run down from his eyes because of those who keep not God's law.

Tzaddi 137–144.　　　　Here he describes the trouble and anguish of his mind. His zeal consumes him because his enemies have forgotten God's words. 'Thy word is very pure : therefore Thy servant loveth it. . . . Thy righteous-ness is an everlasting righteousness, and Thy law is the truth. . . . Give me understanding, and I shall live.'

Koph 145–152.　　　　The Psalmist during a sleepless night contemplated the word of God until the dawning of the morning. He cried with his whole heart : 'Hear me, O Lord, I will keep Thy statutes. . . . Hear my voice accord-ing to Thy lovingkindness : O Lord, quicken me according to Thy judgment.' Those who follow mischief are far from the law. 'Thou art near, O Lord ; . . . . Thy commandments are truth.'

Resh 153–160.　　　　He complains of his many persecutors and enemies, yet he is more grieved because of their neglect of the word of God : 'They seek not Thy statutes.' He prays for the quickening of his spirit—'according to Thy lovingkindness. Thy word is true from the beginning : and every one of Thy righteous judgments endureth for ever.'

Schin 161–168.　　　　Princes have persecuted him for no cause, but he finds his conso-lation and joy in God. He abhors falsehood, but loves the law of God. Seven times a day he praises God. 'Great peace have they that love Thy law, and nothing shall offend them.'

Tau 169–176.　　　　The Psalmist prays for understanding, for the law of God is his delight. He says : 'Let my soul live, and it shall praise Thee. . . . My tongue shall speak of Thy word : for all Thy commandments are right-eousness.' In conclusion he prays these words : 'Seek Thy servant ; for I do not forget Thy commandments.'

Psalm CXX

(*Seven Verses*)

In these verses the Psalmist meditates in distress of mind but he has not sought God in vain, for when he cried unto the Lord the Lord heard him.   He prays for deliverance from 'lying lips' and from a 'deceitful tongue,' which he compares to 'sharp arrows' and 'coals of juniper,' saying, 'I am for peace : but when I speak, they are for war.'

1
2

4

7

Parallel Verses

'Out of the abundance of my complaint and grief have I spoken hitherto.'

1 Sam. i. 16.

' Peace, peace to him that is far off, and to him that is near, saith the Lord ; and I will heal him.   But the wicked are like the troubled sea, when it cannot rest, whose waters cast up mire and dirt.'

Isa. lvii. 19.
Isa. lvii. 20.

' There is no peace, saith my God, to the wicked.'

Isa. lvii. 21.

Psalm CXXI

(*Eight Verses*)

Verses

The Psalmist lifts up his eyes to the hills, whence cometh his help.

1

His help has come from God, ' which made heaven and earth.'   God neither slumbers nor sleeps, but is as a shade from the sun by day and the moon by night.   Hence it is that the Psalmist says, ' He shall preserve thy soul, ... thy going out and thy coming in from this time and for evermore.'

2

3, 4, 5

6, 7

8

Parallel Verses

' . . . . Let not your hearts faint : fear not, and do not tremble, neither be ye terrified ; for the Lord your God is He that goeth with you, ... to save you.'

Deut. xx. 3.
Deut. xx. 4.

' Be strong and of a good courage : fear not, nor be afraid ; . . . . for the Lord thy God, He it is that doth go with Thee ; He will not fail thee, nor forsake thee.'

Deut. xxxi. 6.

' Believe in the Lord your God, so shall ye be established.'

2 Chron. xx. 20.

Psalm CXXII

(Nine Verses)

This is an expression of joy on entering the Temple of Jerusalem,
3, 4 ... a 'city that is compact together : whither the tribes go up, ...
5   to give thanks unto the name of the Lord.   For there are set thrones
6   of judgment, the thrones of the house of David.   Pray for the peace
7   of Jerusalem. ... Peace be within thy walls.   For my brethren
8   and companions' sakes, I will now say, Peace be within thee.   Because
9   of the house of the Lord our God I will seek thy good.'

PARALLEL VERSES

1 Kings ii. 1.   'Now the days of David drew nigh that he should die ; and he
charged Solomon his son saying, I go the way of all the earth : be thou
strong therefore, and shew thyself a man.'

1 Kings ii. 10.   '. . . . So David slept with his fathers, and was buried in the city of
David. ... Seven years he reigned in Hebron and thirty-three years
in Jerusalem.'

1 Kings ii. 12.   'Then sat Solomon upon the throne of David his father.'

1 Kings ii. 45.   'King Solomon shall be blessed, and the throne of David shall be
established before the Lord for ever.'

1 Kings viii.   (When Solomon consecrated the Temple in Jerusalem he said,) 'It
17, 18   was in the heart of David my father to build an house for the name of
the Lord God of Israel.   And the Lord said unto David my father,
Whereas it was in thine heart to build an house unto My name, thou
didst well that it was in thine heart.'

Isaiah lvi. 6.   'Also the sons of the stranger that join themselves to the Lord, to
serve Him, and to love the name of the Lord, to be His servants, ...

Isaiah lvi. 7.   Even them will I bring to My holy mountain, and make them joyful
in My house of prayer   for Mine house shall be called an house
of prayer for all people.'

Psalm CXXIII

(Four Verses)   Verses

The Psalmist lifts up his eyes unto the heavens in prayer to God—   1
He prays for mercy against the contempt and scorning of the proud.   2, 3 4

Parallel Verses

'Thine eyes are upon the haughty, that Thou mayst bring them   2 Sam. xxii. 28.
down.'

'Look on every one that is proud, and abase him.'   Job xi. 12.

'When pride cometh, then cometh shame.'   Prov. xi. 2.

Psalm CXXIV

(Eight Verses)   Verses

The Psalmist speaks in the name of Israel. 'If it had not been the   1, 2
Lord who was on our side, when men rose up against us : . . . . when
their wrath was kindled against us'—then should we have been over-   3, 4
whelmed. 'Blessed be the Lord, who hath not given us as a prey to   6
their teeth. . . . The snare is broken. . .   Our help is in the name of   7, 8
the Lord, who made heaven and earth.'

Parallel Verses

'And Moses told Aaron all the words of the Lord who had sent   Ex. iv. 28.
him.'

'And Moses and Aaron went, and gathered together all the elders   Ex. iv. 29.
of the children of Israel.'

'And Aaron spake all the words which the Lord had spoken unto   Ex. iv. 30.
Moses.'

'And the people believed : and when they heard that the Lord had   Ex. iv. 31.
visited the children of Israel, and that He had looked upon their affliction, then they bowed their heads, and worshipped.'

Psalm CXXV

(Five Verses)

Verses

1	Those who trust in God are compared to Mount Zion, which cannot
2	be removed, but abideth for ever.　For the Lord is round about
3	His people, as the mountains are round about Jerusalem for ever.
4	'The rod of the wicked shall not rest upon the lot of the righteous.'
5	The Psalmist prays that God will bless the upright in heart.

Parallel Verses

Prov. iii. 5.　'Trust in the Lord with all thine heart.'

Prov. iii. 6.　'In all thy ways acknowledge Him, and He shall direct thy paths.'

Prov. iii. 26.　'For the Lord shall be thy confidence, and shall keep thy foot from being taken.'

Prov. iv. 26.　'Ponder the path of thy feet.'

Prov. iv. 27.　'Turn not to the right hand, nor to the left : remove thy foot from evil.'

Psalm CXXVI

(Six Verses)

Verses

	This is a joyous hymn of praise to God for deliverance from the
1	'captivity of Zion.' It was like a dream ;　　they laughed and sang
2	for joy ; 'The Lord hath done great things for them.' Truly were
5	they made to feel that those who 'sow in tears shall reap in joy. . . .
6	He that . . . . weepeth, bearing precious seed, shall doubtless come again with rejoicing, bringing his sheaves with him.'

Parallel Verses

Deut. xxvi. 11.　'And thou shalt rejoice in every good thing, which the Lord thy God hath given unto thee, and unto thine house, thou, and the Levite, and the stranger that is among you.'

1 Sam. xix. 5.　'And the Lord wrought a great salvation for all Israel : thou sawest it, and didst rejoice.'

Isa. lxv. 19.　'I will rejoice in Jerusalem, and joy in my people,' &c.

Psalm CXXVII

(*Five Verses*)

Here the Psalmist teaches the great truth that all labour is in vain without faith and trust in God. Let our children be inheritors of a perfect faith in God, and we shall have God's blessing in them, and we shall never be ashamed. 'Happy is the man that hath his quiver full of them.'

PARALLEL VERSES

'Abraham shall surely become a great and mighty nation, and all Gen. xviii. 18, 19.
the nations of the earth shall be blessed in him. For I know him, that he will command his children and his household after him, and they shall keep the way of the Lord, to do justice and judgment; that the Lord may bring upon Abraham that which He hath spoken of him.'

'Thou shalt love the Lord thy God; . . . . and these words Deut. vi. 5.
shall be in thine heart, and thou shalt teach them diligently unto thy children.'

Psalm CXXVIII

(*Six Verses*)

This is a description of the blessings of those who live in the fear of God, and walk in His ways. Thus the wife is said to be as a fruitful 'vine' and the children like 'olive plants.' 'The Lord shall bless thee out of Zion.' 'Thou shalt see the good of Jerusalem,' and 'thou shalt see thy children's children, and peace upon Israel.'

PARALLEL VERSES

'Thus saith the Lord of hosts, the God of Israel, Amend your ways Jer. vii. 3.
and your doings.'

' If ye thoroughly amend your ways and your doings : if ye Jer. vii. 5.
thoroughly execute judgment between a man and his neighbour.
Then will I cause you to dwell in this place in the land that I gave Jer. vii. 7.
to your fathers, for ever and ever.'

'The Lord will not suffer the soul of the righteous to famish.' Prov. x. 3.

H

Prov. x. 6, 7.   'Blessings are upon the head of the just : . . . . the memory oı the just is blessed.'

Prov. x. 9.   'He that walketh uprightly walketh surely.'

Psalm CXXIX

(*Eight Verses*)

Verses

ı   The afflictions of the house of Israel are here spoken of, yet 'they
2   have not prevailed against me,' because 'the Lord is righteous.' The
4   Psalmist expresses his indignation against the haters of 'Zion.'

PARALLEL VERSES

Isa. li. 15.   'I am the Lord thy God, that divided the sea whose waves roared ·
the Lord of hosts is His name.'

Isa. lii. 1.   'Awake, awake ! put on thy strength, O Zion, put on the beautiful
garments, O Jerusalem, the Holy City.'

Isa. lii. 6, 13.   'My people shall know My name ; My servant shall be exalted and
extolled, and be very high.'

Isa. liii. 2.   . He grew up as a tender plant, as a root out of a dry
ground.'

Isa. liii. 7.   '   He was oppressed and afflicted.'

Isa. liv. 4, 7.   'Fear not ; for thou shalt not be ashamed : . . . . with great mercies

Isa. liv. 14.   will I gather thee. . . . In righteousness shalt thou be established.'

Isa. liv. 17.   'This is the heritage of the servants of the Lord.'

Psalm CXXX

(*Eight Verses*)

Verses

This is an outpouring of anguish from the depths of the soul. Yet
5   the suppliant revives in his perfect faith in God. He says, 'I wait
for the Lord, my soul doth wait, and in His word do I hope.' He
watches for the realisation of his faith, with the same expectation as those
6   who watch for the morning. 'I say, more than they that watch for the
7   morning.' 'Let Israel hope in the Lord : for with the Lord there ıs
8   mercy, and with Him is plenteous redemption. And He shall redeem
Israel from all his iniquities.'

'When my soul fainted within me I remembered the Lord : and my Jonah ii. 7.
prayer came in unto Thee, into Thine holy temple.'

'   Blessed are all they that wait for Him.'   Isa. xxx. 18.

'O Lord, be gracious unto us : we have waited for Thee,   our Isa. xxxiii. 2.
salvation in the time of trouble.'

'Fear ye not, stand still, and see the salvation of the Lord.'   Exodus xiv. 13.

'The Lord liveth, that hath redeemed my soul out of all distress.'   1 Kings i. 29.

Psalm CXXXI
(*Three Verses*)   Verses

An expression of humility : 'Lord, my heart is not haughty. .   I   1
have quieted myself as a child that is weaned of his mother.
Let Israel hope in the Lord from henceforth and for ever.'

'The fear of the Lord is to hate evil : pride and arrogancy . . .   do Prov. viii. 13.
I hate.'

'When pride cometh, then cometh shame.'   Prov. xi. 2.

'Only by pride cometh contention.'   Prov. xiii. 10.

'Every one that is proud in heart is an abomination to the Lord.'   Prov. xvi. 5.

'Pride goeth before destruction, and a haughty spirit before a fall.'   Prov. xvi. 18.

'Before destruction the heart of man is haughty.'   Prov. xviii. 12.

'A high look and a proud heart . . . . is sin.'   Prov. xxi. 4.

'A man's pride shall bring him low.'   Prov. xxix. 23.

'For thus saith the high and lofty One that inhabiteth eternity,
whose name is Holy ; I dwell in the high and holy place, with him also
that is of a contrite and humble spirit, to revive the spirit of the humble,
and to revive the heart of the contrite ones.'   Isaiah lvii. 15.

Psalm CXXXII
(*Eighteen Verses*)   Verses

'Lord, remember David and all his afflictions : how he sware unto   1, 2
the Lord, and vowed unto the mighty God of Jacob,' that he will   4

Verses
9
11

13, 14

17

18

give himself no rest until he finds a resting-place for the ark of God. The Psalmist prays that the priests may be 'clothed with righteousness,' that God's saints may 'shout for joy.' 'The Lord hath sworn in truth to David, ... Of the fruit of thy body will I set upon thy throne.   For the Lord hath chosen Zion ; this is My rest for ever   There will I make the horn of David to bud : I have ordained a lamp for Mine anointed.' His enemies will be clothed 'with shame : but upon himself shall his crown flourish.'

PARALLEL VERSES

2 Sam. vii. 1.   'And it came to pass, when the king sat in his house, and the Lord had given him rest round about from all his enemies ; that the

2 Sam. vii. 2.   king said unto Nathan the prophet, See now, I dwell in a house of cedar, but the ark of God dwelleth within curtains.'

2 Sam. vii. 3.   'And Nathan said to the king, Go, do all that is in thine heart ; for the Lord is with thee.'

2 Sam. vii. 8.   '   Thus saith the Lord of hosts, I took thee from the sheep-cote, from following the sheep, to be ruler over My people, over Israel. . . .'

2 Sam. vii. 12.   'And when thy days be fulfilled, and thou shalt sleep with thy fathers, I will set up thy seed after thee. . . .'

2 Sam. vii. 13.   'He shall build a house for My name, and I will establish the throne of his kingdom for ever.'

2 Sam. vii. 27.   '. . . . Thou, O Lord of hosts God of Israel, hast revealed to Thy servant, saying, I will build thee an house : therefore hath Thy servant found in his heart to pray this prayer unto Thee.'

2 Sam. vii. 28.   'And now, O Lord God, Thou art that God, and Thy words be true, and Thou hast promised this goodness unto Thy servant.'

2 Sam. vii. 29.   With Thy blessing let the house of Thy servant be blessed for ever.'

Psalm CXXXIII

Verses

(Three Verses)

2

3

In poetical language the Psalmist describes the beauty of family unity. He compares it to the anointing oil of the priesthood ; for there 'the Lord commanded the blessing, even life for evermore.'

PARALLEL VERSES

'And Abram said unto Lot, Let there be no strife, I pray thee, Gen. xiii. 8.
between me and thee ; . . . . for we be brethren.'

'Thou shalt not hate thy brother in thine heart.' Lev. xix. 17.

'Thou shalt open thine hand wide unto thy brother, to thy poor, Deut. xv. 11.
and to thy needy, in thy land.'

'Pleasant words are as an honeycomb, sweet to the soul, and health Prov. xvi. 24.
to the bones.'

'Better is a dry morsel and quietness therewith, than a house full of Prov. xvii. 1.
sacrifice with strife.'

'The beginning of strife is as when one letteth out water.' Prov. xvii. 14.

'It is an honour for a man to cease from strife.' Prov. xx. 3.

'The just man walketh in his integrity : his children are blessed Prov. xx. 7.
after him.'

Psalm CXXXIV

(*Three Verses*)

Verses

'Bless ye the Lord, all ye servants of the Lord.   Lift up your   1, 2
hands in the sanctuary, and bless the Lord. The Lord that made   3
heaven and earth, bless thee out of Zion.'

PARALLEL VERSE

'And Ezra blessed the Lord, the great God. And all the people Neh. viii. 6.
answered, Amen, Amen, with lifting up their hands : and they bowed
their heads, and worshipped the Lord, with their faces to the ground.'

Psalm CXXXV

(*Twenty-one Verses*)

NOTE.—See Psalm 115 (Eighteen Verses).

This Psalm (135) is almost identical with the 115th. It contains
an indignant protest against idolatry, and dwells on the great contrast between the worship of idols and the worship of Almighty God.

Verses   The Psalmist refers to the wonders of nature—in 'heaven' and 'earth,' in the 'seas' and 'deep places'—vapours that ascend from the earth, rain, wind, and lightning—and he alludes to the Redemption. God gave them the land of Canaan, 'an heritage unto Israel His people . . . .

13   throughout all generations !' 'Thy name, O Lord, endureth for ever.' The Psalmist concludes with an appeal to the house of Israel, Aaron,

21   and Levi. 'Blessed be the Lord out of Zion, which dwelleth at Jerusalem. Praise ye the Lord.'

PARALLEL VERSES

1 Chron. xvi. 4.   'And he (David) appointed certain of the Levites to minister before the ark of the Lord, and to record, and to thank and praise the Lord God of Israel.'

1 Chron. xvi. 7.   'Then on that day David delivered first this Psalm to thank the Lord into the hand of Asaph and his brethren.'

1 Chron. xvi. 8.   'Give thanks unto the Lord: call upon His name.' (See Psalm 105.)

Psalm CXXXVI

(*Twenty-six Verses*)

Verses   In this famous hymn of praise and thanksgiving is summarised the history of Israel, through the several stages of their deliverance from the Egyptian bondage, when, 'with a strong hand' and a

11
12   'stretched out arm,' God brought out Israel ; 'for His mercy endureth for ever.' And He made Israel to pass through the Red Sea, and over-threw Pharaoh and his host ; but He gave an 'heritage' unto 'Israel

15, 22   His servant,' and remembered them in their low estate, and redeemed

23, 24   them from their enemies—and 'giveth food to all flesh.' 'O give

25, 26   thanks unto the God of heaven : for His mercy endureth for ever.'

PARALLEL VERSES

Exodus xii. 40.   'Now the sojourning of the children of Israel, who dwelt in Egypt, was four hundred and thirty years.'

Exodus xii. 41.   'And it came to pass at the end of the four hundred and thirty years, even the self-same day, it came to pass that all the hosts of the Lord went out from the land of Egypt.'

It is a night to be much observed unto the Lord for bringing them   Exodus xii. 42.
out from the land of Egypt : this is that night of the Lord to be observed
of all the children of Israel in their generations.'

'And Moses said unto the people, Remember this day, in which   Exodus xiii. 3.
ye came out of Egypt, out of the house of bondage : for by strength of
hand the Lord brought you out from this place.'

Psalm CXXXVII
(*Nine Verses*)

Verses

This pathetic Psalm describes in graphic language the heart-broken
sorrow of the captives who were taken from their own dear land to Babylon. There they sat down and wept when they remembered Zion. They   1
hung their harps upon the willows. Those who had carried them away   3
captives asked them to sing ' one of the songs of Zion.' They replied,
' How shall we sing the Lord's song in a strange land ? ' They swore faith-   4
fulness to Jerusalem, and bitterly reproached the daughters of Babylon.   8

PARALLEL VERSES

' In the third year of the reign of Jehoiakim, king of Judah, came   Dan. i. 1.
Nebuchadnezzar, King of Babylon, unto Jerusalem, and besieged it. . . .'
Among the captives taken to Babylon were Daniel, Shadrach, Meshach,
and Abednego. . . .

' Turn Thou us unto Thee, O Lord, and we shall be turned ; renew   Lam. v. 5.
our days as of old.'

Psalm CXXXVIII
(*Eight Verses*)

Verses

The Psalmist pours out his 'whole heart' to God in prayer. He   1
calls to mind the day when he cried and found an answer in strength of   3
soul. ' Though the Lord be high, yet hath He respect unto the lowly :   6
but the proud He knoweth afar off.' So great is his faith that although   7
he walks in the midst of trouble, he exclaims, ' Thou wilt revive me. ·

The Lord will perfect that which concerneth me : Thy mercy, O Lord, endureth for ever : forsake not the works of Thine own hands.'

PARALLEL VERSES

Isa. xxxviii. 1.   It is recorded in this chapter that when King Hezekiah had been
Isa. xxxviii. 2. 'sick unto death,' he turned his face toward the wall, and prayed unto
Isa. xxxviii. 4. the Lord.   Then came the word of the Lord to Isaiah, saying, Go and
Isa. xxxviii. 5. say to Hezekiah, Thus saith the Lord, the God of David thy father, I
Isa. xxxviii. 9. have heard thy prayer and seen thy tears. . . . After he had recove·ed
Isa. xxxviii. 19. of his sickness, he said, 'The living, the living, he shall praise Thee, as
I do this day : the father to the children shall make known Thy truth.'
Hab. iii. 2.   'O Lord, revive Thy work in the midst of the years.'

Psalm CXXXIX

(*Twenty-four Verses*)

\erses

This superb Psalm is a contemplation of the presence and immanence

1   of God in relation to the individual.   'O Lord, Thou hast searched me,

2, 3   and known me. . . . Thou understandest my thought. . . . Thou com-
passest my path and my lying down, and art acquainted with all my
ways.'   The omnipresence of God is here demonstrated in striking

7   language.   'Whither shall I go from Thy spirit? or whither shall I flee
from Thy presence?'   There comes an outburst of thanksgiving.   'I

14   will praise Thee ; for I am fearfully and wonderfully made : marvellous
are Thy works ; and that my soul knoweth right well.'   Then follows a

22   cry of righteous indignation against the wicked : 'I count them mine
enemies ;' and finally a prayer for deliverance from sin, and to be led 'in

24   the way everlasting.'

PARALLEL VERSES

Exodus xxxiii.   ' My presence shall go with thee, and I will give thee rest.'
14.
1 Chron. xxviii.   'The Lord searcheth all hearts, and understandeth all the imagina-
9.   tions of the thoughts ; if thou seek Him, He will be found of thee.'

Isa. xliii. 3.   'When thou passest through the waters, I will be with thee ; and
through the rivers, they shall not overflow thee : when thou walkest
through the fire, thou shalt not be burned ; neither shall the flame
kindle upon thee.'

'Hast thou not known? hast thou not heard, that the everlasting Isa. xl. 28. God, the Lord, the creator of the ends of the earth, fainteth not, neither is weary? there is no searching of His understanding.'

Psalm CXL

(*Thirteen Verses*)

Verses

This is a fervent prayer for protection against the 'evil' and 1 'violent' man, in whose heart is 'mischief,' and whose 'tongue' is like 2 that of a 'serpent.' The Psalmist finds 'strength' and 'hope' in his 3, 4 great faith. 'O God the Lord, the strength of my salvation, Thou 7 hast covered my head in the day of battle. . . . Let not an evil speaker 11 be established in the earth.' He knows that God will maintain the 12 cause of the afflicted and the right of the poor. 'Surely the righteous shall give thanks unto Thy name: the upright shall dwell in Thy 13 presence.'

PARALLEL VERSES

'He (God) disappointeth the devices of the crafty, so that their Job v. 12. hands cannot perform their enterprise.'

'The spirit of a man will sustain his infirmity.' Prov. xviii. 14.

'There are many devices in a man's heart: nevertheless the counsel Prov. xix. 21. of the Lord, that shall stand.'

Psalm CXLI

(*Ten Verses*)

Verses

This is a Psalm of special ethical value. It is an entreaty for Divine protection against temptation and sin. 'Set a watch, O Lord, 3 before my mouth; keep the door of my lips. Incline not my heart to 4 any evil thing. . . . Let the righteous smite me; it shall be a kindness.' 5

PARALLEL VERSES

'And Asa cried unto the Lord his God, and said, Lord, it is nothing 2 Chron. xiv. 11. with Thee to help, whether with many, or with them that have no power : help us, O Lord our God ; for we rest on Thee, and in Thy name we go against this multitude. O Lord, Thou art our God : let not man prevail against us.'

2 Chron. xv. 4.   ' When they in their trouble did turn unto the Lord God of Israel, and sought Him, He was found of them.'

Psalm CXLII

(Seven Verses)

Verses

^   The Psalmist records that he had poured out his complaint before God. ' I shewed before Him my trouble.' In vain he looked for human
4   help. No man cared for his soul, but when his spirit was overwhelmed
5   within him God knew his path. ' I cried unto Thee, O Lord : I said, Thou art my refuge and my portion in the land of the living.
7   Thou shalt deal bountifully with me.'

PARALLEL VERSES

Hab. iii. 17, 18, 19.   ' Although the fig tree shall not blossom, neither shall fruit be in the vines ; the labour of the olive shall fail, and the fields shall yield no meat ; the flock shall be cut off from the fold, and there shall be no herd in the stalls : yet I will rejoice in the Lord, I will joy in the God of my salvation. The Lord God is my strength, and He will make my feet like hinds' feet, and He will make me to walk upon mine high places.'

Zech. iv. 6.   '   Not by might, nor by power, but by My spirit, saith the Lord of hosts.'

Psalm CXLIII

(Twelve Verses)

Verses

*   In deepest anguish of mind the Psalmist appeals to God : ' In Thy
4   faithfulness,' and in Thy ' righteousness ' answer me ! His ' spirit is overwhelmed,' his heart is desolate. He meditates on the works of
5, 6   God. ' My soul thirsteth after Thee, as a thirsty land.' As in the twenty-eighth Psalm he says again, ' Hear me speedily, O Lord : my spirit faileth :
7   hide not Thy face from me, lest I be like unto them that go down into
8   the pit. Cause me to hear Thy lovingkindness in the morning ; for in

Thee do I trust : cause me to know the way wherein I should walk ; for I lift up my soul unto Thee. . . . Teach me to do Thy will ; for Thou art my God : Thy spirit is good ; lead me into the land of uprightness. Quicken me, O Lord, for Thy name's sake : for Thy righteousness' sake bring my soul out of trouble.'

PARALLEL VERSES

'Mine eyes fail with looking upward : O Lord, I am oppressed ; Isa. xxxviii. 14. undertake for me.'

The everlasting God, the Lord, the Creator of the ends of Isa. xl. 28. the earth, fainteth not, neither is weary ; there is no searching of His understanding. He giveth power to the faint; and to them that have no might He increaseth strength. Even the youths shall faint and be weary, and the young men shall utterly fall : but they that wait upon the Lord shall renew their strength ; they shall mount up with wings as eagles ; they shall run, and not be weary ; and they shall walk, and not faint.'

'Do not I fill heaven and earth ? saith the Lord.' Jer. xxiii. 24.

Psalm CXLIV

(*Fifteen Verses*)

Verses

The Psalmist blesses God who has been his 'strength,' his 'good- 1 ness,' his 'fortress,' his 'high tower,' his 'shield,' and his 'deliverer' 2 in whom he trusts. He meditates upon the conditions of man's life 3, 4 on earth. He says, 'Man is like to vanity ; his days are as a shadow that passeth away.' He prays, 'Deliver me out of great waters, from 7, 11 the hand of strange children.' In the midst of these prayers and meditations he sings a 'new song' upon a psaltery and an 'instru- 9 ment of ten strings'; he prays again for the prosperity of 'sons' 12 and 'daughters,' for an increase of 'stores,' and perfect peace, 'that 13, 14 there be no complaining in our streets,' and finally exclaims, ' Happy is that people, that is in such a case : yea, happy is that people, whose 15 God is the Lord.'

PARALLEL VERSES

Gen. xix. 19.   'Behold now, Thy servant hath found grace in Thy sight; and Thou hast magnified Thy mercy, which Thou hast shewed unto me in saving my life.'

Exodus xxxiii. 18, 19.   'And he (Moses) said, I beseech Thee, shew me Thy glory. And He said, I will make all My goodness pass before thee, and I will proclaim the name of the Lord before thee ; and will be gracious to whom I will be gracious, and will shew mercy on whom I will shew mercy.'

Jer. ix. 23.   'Thus saith the Lord, Let not the wise man glory in his wisdom, neither let the mighty man glory in his might, let not the rich man glory in his riches.'

Jer. ix. 24.   'But let him that glorieth glory in this, that he understandeth and knoweth Me, that I am the Lord that exercise lovingkindness, judgment, and righteousness in the earth ; for in these things I delight, saith the Lord.'

Psalm CXLV

(*Twenty-one Verses*)

Verses

1   This Psalm is the culmination of praise and worship. 'I will extol
2   Thee, my God, O King ; and I will bless Thy name for ever and ever.' Day by day the Psalmist declares God's 'greatness,' which is 'unsearchable,' His 'compassion,' God's 'tender mercies' over all His works ;
4   that 'one generation' shall praise His works to another. 'Slow to anger,'
9   of 'great mercy, the Lord is good to all.   To make known to the
12, 13   sons of men' that His 'kingdom is an everlasting kingdom,' 'endureth
14, 15   throughout all generations.' 'He upholdeth all that fall.' Hence it is that the eyes of all 'wait' upon Him. He satisfies the desire of every
16   living thing. 'The Lord is nigh unto all that call upon Him . . . in
18, 21   truth.' He will hear their cry, and save them. 'Let all flesh bless His holy name for ever and ever.'

PARALLEL VERSES

Jer. x. 1.   'Hear ye the word which the Lord speaketh unto you, O house of Israel.   '

Jer. x. 6.   'Forasmuch as there is none like unto Thee, O Lord; Thou art great, and Thy name is great in might.'

'Who would not fear thee, O King of nations? for to Thee doth Jer. x. 7.
it appertain: forasmuch as among all the wise men of the nations, and
in all their kingdoms, there is none like unto Thee. . . .'

'The Lord is the true God, He is the living God, and an everlasting Jer. x. 10.
King.

'He hath made the earth by His power, He hath established the Jer. x. 12.
world by His wisdom, and hath stretched out the heavens by His
discretion. . . .'

'The Lord of hosts is His name.' Jer. x. 16.

'It is not in man that walketh to direct his steps.' Jer. x. 23.

'The Lord, the Lord God, merciful and gracious, long-suffering and Exodus xxxiv.
abundant in goodness and truth, keeping mercy for thousands, forgiving 6, 7.
iniquity and transgression and sin.'

The last five Psalms are joyous hymns of praise, commencing with
the same phrase, 'Praise ye the Lord'; but each of them contains distinct
reflections suggested by the spirit of thanksgiving.

Psalm CXLVI

(*Ten Verses*)

Verses

The Psalmist declares that whilst he has his being he will sing   1
praises to God. He warns his fellow-men against trust in princes or   2
in the 'son of man,' in whom there is no power; but happy is he   3
whose hope is in the 'Lord his God,' who made heaven and earth, the   4
sea, and 'keepeth truth for ever.' God 'executeth judgment for the   5
oppressed,' 'giveth food to the hungry,' 'looseth the prisoners,'   6
'openeth the eyes of the blind,' 'raiseth them that are bowed   7
down,' 'loveth the righteous,' and 'preserveth the strangers.' 'He   8
relieveth the fatherless and widow.' 'The Lord shall reign for ever,   9
even Thy God, O Zion, unto all generations.'   10

PARALLEL VERSES

'Thou hast been a strength to the poor, a strength to the needy in Isa. xxv. 4.
his distress, a refuge from the storm, a shadow from the heat.'

'For a small moment have I forsaken thee: but with great mercies Isa. liv. 7.
will I gather thee. With everlasting kindness will I have mercy on Isa. liv. 8.
thee, saith the Lord thy Redeemer.'

Isa. liv. 10. ' The mountains shall depart, and the hills be removed ; but My kindness shall not depart from thee, neither shall the covenant of My peace be removed, saith the Lord that hath mercy on thee.'

Isa. liv. 13. 'And all thy children shall be taught of the Lord ; and great shall be the peace of thy children.'

Isa. liv. 14. 'In righteousness shalt thou be established : thou shalt be far from oppression ; for thou shalt not fear : and from terror ; for it shall not come near thee.'

Psalm CXLVII

(*Twenty Verses*)

Verses

· 'It is good to sing praises unto our God ; it is pleasant ' and 'comely.'
2 The Psalmist foreshadows the future of Jerusalem, when the out-
3 casts of Israel will be gathered together. The broken-hearted will be
5 healed; 'for great is our Lord, ... His understanding is infinite.' He
8 describes the wonders of Nature. The clouds prepare rain for the
11 earth. 'The Lord taketh pleasure in them that fear Him,' and who
12 'hope in His mercy. Praise the Lord, O Jerusalem ; praise thy God,
13, 14 O Zion. He hath blessed thy children within thee,' and ' maketh
15 peace in thy borders. He sendeth forth His commandment upon
19 earth : His word runneth very swiftly. . . . He sheweth His word unto Jacob, His statutes and His judgments unto Israel. He hath not
20 dealt so with any nation : and as for His judgments, they have not known them. Praise ye the Lord.'

PARALLEL VERSES

Exodus xv. 11. 'Who is like unto thee, O Lord, among the gods ? Who is like Thee, glorious in holiness, fearful in praises, doing wonders ? '

Exodus xv. 17. 'Thou shalt bring them in, and plant them in the mountain of Thine inheritance, in the place which Thou hast made for Thee to dwell in, in the sanctuary, O Lord, which Thy hands have established.'

Exodus xv. 18. 'The Lord shall reign for ever and ever.'

Deut. iv. 39. 'Know therefore this day, and consider it in thine heart, that the Lord He is God in heaven above, and upon the earth beneath ; there is none else.'

Psalm CXLVIII

(*Fourteen Verses*)

Here is a general exhortation to all mankind, to the heavens above, and to the earth beneath, to praise and worship God : to the 'kings of the earth, and all people,' to 'princes and all judges of the earth :   11 both young men and maidens ; old men and children : let them   12 praise the name of the Lord : for His name alone is excellent ; His   13 glory is above the earth and heaven. He also exalteth the horn of   14 His people, the praise of His saints ; even of the children of Israel, a people near unto Him. Praise ye the Lord.'

PARALLEL VERSES

'. . . . Holy, holy, holy is the Lord of hosts ; the whole earth is full Isa. vi. 3. of His glory.'

'Cry out and shout, thou inhabitant of Zion : for great is the Holy Isa. xii. 6. One of Israel in the midst of thee.'

'O Lord, Thou art my God ; I will exalt Thee, I will praise Thy name ; Isa. xxv. 1. for Thou hast done wonderful things ; Thy counsels of old are faithfulness and truth.'

'He will swallow up death in victory : and the Lord God will wipe Isa. xxv. 8. away tears from off all faces ; and the rebuke of His people shall He take away from off all the earth : for the Lord hath spoken it.'

Psalm CXLIX

(*Nine Verses*)

Sing unto the Lord a new song, and His praise in the congregation   1 of saints. Let Israel rejoice in Him that made him : let the children   2 of Zion be joyful in their King.' In the dance, with timbrel and harp,   3 let them praise God. 'Let the saints be joyful in glory : let them   5 sing aloud upon their beds.   Praise ye the Lord.'

PARALLEL VERSES

'In that day shall this song be sung in the land of Judah : We have Isa. xxvi. 1. a strong city ; salvation will God appoint for walls and bulwarks.'

'Open ye the gates, that the righteous nation which keepeth the Isa. xxvi. 2. truth may enter in.'

Isa. xxvi. 4. 'Trust ye in the Lord for ever : for in the Lord Jehovah is everlasting strength.'

Isa. xxviii. 5. 'In that day shall the Lord of hosts be for a crown of glory and for a diadem of beauty unto the residue of His people.'

Psalm CL

(Six Verses)

Verses

1 'Praise God in His sanctuary'—in the firmament of His power ;
2 for His mighty acts, according to His excellent greatness ; with the
3, 4 sound of the trumpet, with psaltery and harp, with timbrel and dance,
5 with stringed instruments and organs, with loud cymbals, with high
6 sounding cymbals. 'Let every thing that hath breath praise the Lord. Praise ye the Lord.'

Parallel Verses

Isa. xxxviii.19. 'The living, the living, he shall praise Thee, as I do this day.'

Isa. xxix. 19. 'The meek also shall increase their joy in the Lord, and the poor among men shall rejoice in the Holy One of Israel.'

Isa. xxix. 24. 'They also that erred in spirit shall come to understanding, and they that murmured shall learn doctrine.'

Isa. xlii. 10. 'Sing unto the Lord a new song, and His praise from the end of the earth, ye that go down to the sea, and all that is therein : the isles, and the inhabitants thereof.'

Isa. xlii. 12. 'Let them give glory unto the Lord, and declare His praise in the islands.'

Thus ends the matchless collection of devotional exercises known as the Psalter. They meet the needs of human nature in all its varied moods of joy, of sorrow, of repentance, of faith and hope. This Divine faith is the keynote of the entire collection. It is a faith which is taught by the people of Israel, and is destined to become the universal possession of every human heart.

Spottiswoode & Co. Printers, New-Street Square, London

CPSIA information can be obtained at www.ICGtesting.com
Printed in the USA
BVOW06s1528181215

430601BV00027B/613/P